MAROONED

The story of a Cornish seaman

James Derriman

British Library Cataloguing in Publication Data
Derriman, James P. Derriman
Marooned: the story of a Cornish seaman.
   1. Great Britain, Royal Navy, Jeffery, Robert
   1. Title
   358.338092

ISBN 978-09549137 7 9

First edition published 1991 by Kenneth Mason.
Second edition published 2006 by
Polperro Heritage Press,
Clifton-upon-Teme, Worcestershire WR6 6EN UK
www.polperropress.co.uk

Cover design
Sue Lord

Printed by Orphans Press
Leominster HR6 8JT UK

Contents

Illustrations

Preface to Second Edition

In the fifteen years since this book first appeared the remote island of Sombrero has become much better known. I first came across the story of Robert Jeffery in the pages of Couch's *History of Polperro*, now a rare book and recently reprinted in facsimile by Polperro Heritage Press. Naval historians and others have written about it, but so far *Marooned* remains the first and probably the only book to embody detailed research on this remarkable episode. (One review, in a Canadian maritime publication, charmingly referred to 'Derriman, whose credo, like Jacky Fisher, seems to be that of the mole: he may be traced by his upheavals'!)

When *Marooned* was written the internet was in its infancy. Now, if you put the words 'Sombrero + Island' into the Google search engine, it will produce for you many hundreds of web sites. A proposal to make Sombrero into a rocket-launching site arose, and (I think happily) came to nothing. Its outstanding wildlife has been studied by scientists, and drawn the attention of conservationists. The sea-birds and the endemic black lizards have the tiny, barren isle to themselves again.

Meanwhile my little book attracted some readers, and became the basis of an exhibition in the excellent local museum at Polperro, Jeffery's birthplace. Now it is out of print, and I felt that a new edition, with a very few revisions, might be justified. My friend Jeremy Rowett Johns, himself with many historical links to Polperro, offered to oblige. So here it is.

JPD
March 2006

Foreword

The young Cornish seaman Robert Jeffery was marooned by his captain on a desolate tropical island, without food or water, in 1807. It was almost three years before he was found alive and living in Massachusetts, having been rescued by an American schooner. When the episode first became known to the British public in 1810 it caused a sensation in Parliament and the Press. At intervals since then it has been re-discovered and written about, then forgotten again: but never fully researched. Unpublished material in the Admiralty papers at the Public Record Office, Kew and in the Whitbread Papers at the Bedfordshire Record Office, has made it possible to learn much more of this strange case, and disclosed some unexpected and entertaining sidelights. Meanwhile an authoritative recent study, *Crime and Punishment in the Royal Navy (Discipline on the Leeward Islands Station 1784-1812)*, (Gower Press, 1989) by John D. Byrn, Jr has quoted the episode in its specialised context, as an example of inhumanity unusual even for its period.

Thus no apology is needed for telling the story afresh, and its dramatic quality has not lessened with the lapse of time. The case occurred at an opportune moment. Such a publicised example of cruelty drew attention to the plight of seamen in the Royal Navy of Nelson's day. While praised at home for their bravery, they had to live and work in appalling conditions at sea, under officers who could all too easily abuse their autocratic powers, especially in wartime.

In writing this book I have received generous help from many people, including Dr. N. A. M. Rodger and the staff of the Public Record Office at Kew; the staff of the Bedfordshire Record Office; Mrs M. Gosling and her colleagues of the Marblehead Historical Society, Massachusetts; and Miss E. Fountain, librarian of the Essex Institute, Salem, Massachusetts.

Quotations from documents at the Public Record Office appear by permission of the Controller of Her Majesty's Stationery Office; and items from the Whitbread Papers by permission of S. C. Whitbread, Esq.

Publication of this book has been assisted by a grant from The Twenty Seven Foundation administered by the Institute of Historical Research, University of London. My wife, as always, has been my most valued critic and a constant source of patient back-up in countless ways.

James P Derriman, 1991

Chapter 1

THE ISLAND OF DOOM

Robert Jeffery, the Cornish boy who was to become the victim of a scandalous episode of English naval history, was born on December 11, 1789 at Fowey.[1]   Whenever England was at war with France, privateers used that historic little seaport, then the busiest in Cornwall, bar Falmouth. They, and naval vessels patrolling the Channel, brought in many a valuable prize. Smugglers, too, were prospering in proportion to the reduction of normal trade by the war. It was enough to catch the imagination of any lad.

The oldest of the four children of John Jeffery, a bargeman, and his wife Honor, Robert spent his early boyhood among the narrow streets by the busy Fowey river. In 1796 the family moved to Polperro, six miles east along the coast, where his father took a public-house.[2]

Polperro, with its small harbour flanked by steep hills and almost hidden from seaward, was still a remote fishing village, whose people spoke a dialect hard even for their fellow-Cornishmen to understand. Just then it was enjoying more prosperity than before or since, as headquarters for privateers and smuggling gangs - quite apart from some legitimate seaborne trade in grain and pilchards. We do not know which was John Jeffery's tavern, but there were, and are, many from which to choose.

Young Robert was sent away to school at Looe - probably West Looe, three miles east of Polperro. No doubt he lived with a relative, and attended Speccott's charity school founded to instruct poor children 'in the mathematics, particularly in those branches which relate to navigation'.[3] His master was a Mr Parnell.

When Robert was 12 his father died and the boy left school already better educated than many of his elders, to return to Polperro where literacy was far from universal.[4] His own mother signed the Talland parish register with a cross, when almost at once she remarried, on June 21, 1801. Her second husband was a local blacksmith, Benjamin Coad, who used his savings to buy the lease of a plot of land on the west - or Lansallos - side of the village,[5] where he built a cottage and workshop. For the next six years the boy worked in the smithy learning his stepfather's trade. By the time he was 17 the attraction of the sea and adventure was too great. Privateers, often owned in Guernsey or Plymouth, found Polperro a useful port between voyages and a ready source of new hands, lads who at least knew one end of a ship from the other. The privateers needed a large complement to provide crews to work prize vessels into port but in spite of rules about protection and protests to the Admiralty, naval captains found them a ready prey for their press gangs. In August 1807 one of these 'private ships of war', the *Lord Nelson*, anchored off Polperro to wait for hands. This was young Robert's chance, and - probably with other local men and boys - he signed on.[6] His trade as a blacksmith made him welcome as an armourer (though still rated as a seaman).[7]

Slight and fair, with a long serious face and grey eyes, five foot seven tall, he was not a typical Cornish lad in appearance. Nor had he the build of a blacksmith or indeed a seaman, though he was described as a good workman in his stepfather's smithy. The only other physical characteristic which local people remembered about him later was that his left knee bent inwards a little.[8]

The *Lord Nelson* was probably badly in need of seamen. She was a foreign-built square-sterned schooner of nearly 70 tons, no doubt a French prize, armed with eight carriage guns, six- and four-pounders. Yet her complement when her owners applied for her letter of marque was only 16. The *Lord Nelson* soon weighed anchor and sailed along the coast to Falmouth, perhaps to take on stores or in the hope of finding more seamen. By ill-luck, the naval brig-sloop HMS *Recruit* lay there, about to sail for the West Indies, and she too was in need of hands.

The *Recruit*, 383 tons and 18 guns, had been built only the year before. She was one of the small Cruiser class of warships more or less equivalent to the modern corvette. Small warships of this kind were known as sloops but that title referred to their size and function rather than their rig. The *Recruit* was, in fact, a brig. Her official complement was 121, but on August 11, as she lay off Falmouth, she had no more than about 100 men.

A gang was sent aboard the privateer to take what men they could get away with. The *Lord Nelson*'s commander, Francis May, understandably but foolishly remonstrated. For a merchant navy master (letter of marque or no) to answer back a Royal Navy officer was asking for trouble. He got it. As an officer of the *Recruit* recorded in his log under August 11, 1807: 'PM: Boarded the *Lord Nelson* Privateer the Master behaving Insolent Pressed ten Men from her'.[9]

One of those ten men was young Robert Jeffery. By law the navy was allowed to take only men who 'used the sea' and were between the ages of 18 and 55. Little notice was taken of this. Jeffery had 'used the sea' for just three weeks, and was aged only 17. Of the other nine pressed men three were also from Polperro: a 16-year-old boy named Richard Johns, John Johns, aged 40 and John Libby, aged 31. The remaining six included two Plymouth men, William Hitchens and William May (perhaps a relative of the privateer master), an Irishman, Swede, Latvian and Norwegian.

They found themselves joining an unhappy warship, commanded by a petty tyrant, Lieutenant the Honourable Warwick Lake. Moreover it was probably a particularly bad moment to encounter him. Only two days before he had complained to the Admiralty that having chased and caught a smuggling vessel off the Cornish coast and sent boats to seize her crew, the men had been rescued from his grasp by - of all people - a party of Sea Fencibles (local defence volunteers) who put off from the shore and landed the smugglers.

Warwick Lake was the youngest son of General Viscount Lake who had earned an unenviable reputation as a British commander in Ireland. He was criticised for allowing his troops unchecked licence and for his indiscriminate severity in suppressing the rebellion of 1798 which broke out during his brief period as commander-in-chief. After the notorious siege of Vinegar Hill, in County Wexford, he hanged all rebels found with arms, expressing deep regret at the necessity of making examples.

That was now behind him. In this year of 1807 the general had returned to England after service as a most successful commander in India, at first under the future Duke of Wellington and later as commander-in-chief. His policy there had been aggressive and bold, with continuous fierce fighting. His conquests included the cities of Delhi and Agra for which he was awarded a peerage. General Lake, popular with all ranks of his army, and had an outstanding ability to inspire his subordinates.

Now a viscount, he was not wealthy but he and a younger brother held office in the household of the Prince of Wales, later George IV. He was on close terms with the Prince, who was also Duke of Cornwall; he was appointed Receiver-General of the Duchy in which capacity he has been described, unexpectedly, as 'avuncular'.[10] Moreover, a substantial pension of £2,000 was settled to descend to the next two holders of the title. His eldest son Francis Gerard, was a successful soldier who commanded the 1st Life Guards in Sicily; the second son, George, was also a distinguished officer who had served on his father's staff. As a family, the Lakes were on top of the world.

Warwick, the third son, had entered the navy at 15. At 26

he now had his own command, though still only a lieutenant. Today his rank might be lieutenant-commander. His title of captain was by courtesy only. Like him, at least two of the *Recruit's* officers - the second lieutenant, Richard Mould and the master, Edward Spencer - were young men new to their rank.

Two days after Jeffery was brought aboard, and even before the brig left Falmouth, two Royal Marine sentries, a quartermaster and three seamen took the cutter from the stern of the ship and escaped. Technically they were deserters, but 'escape' is how the incident was recorded and how it was regarded on board. Desertion was frequent in the navy of the Napoleonic wars, but in the *Recruit* the number of 'run' men was remarkably high.

The ship sailed for the West Indies to join the Leeward Islands station commanded by Rear-Admiral Sir Alexander Cochrane. After calling briefly at Madeira for wine and provisions she set course across the Atlantic for the Guiana coast, then north to Barbados where she anchored briefly in Carlisle Bay and took on water.

Throughout the voyage the logs indicate that the officers and petty officers had little respect for each other and the crew were unruly. The men were flogged, mostly for the usual offences of drunkenness and disobedience; the petty officers could not be physically punished but from time to time were confined to their cabins.

Sometimes Jeffery suffered under the 'starters' of the boatswain or his mates - the knotted rope's ends with which the seamen were struck on the slightest excuse or none at all. This 'hurt him very much', the master admitted later, as if it were remarkable.

There is no reason to think that Robert Jeffery was either better or worse behaved than most other youths thrust into the rough-and-tumble of service life - and rough in those days it certainly was. It was hardly to be expected that he

13

would escape trouble for long. One day as he was passing the Gunner's cabin he noticed a bottle of rum there and helped himself. As unofficial armourer he might well have been thought to have legitimate reason to go to the Gunner's cabin, and get away with his misdemeanour. Unfortunately for him, he had hardly had time to swallow a mouthful when a midshipman named Graham caught him in the act and reported the incident.[11]

Young Robert was put under arrest and kept in irons for two days - the usual preliminary to a flogging. He was far from the only offender awaiting retribution, and at 10 o'clock on the morning of Saturday, November 21, 1807 all hands were piped on deck to witness punishment. The procedure would have begun with the captain reading the Articles of War before officers and men standing bare-headed. Then Jeffery and seven others were seized up to a grating at the gangway and one after another flogged.[12] All had been found guilty of drunkenness, and all but one (and that one not Jeffery) of 'disobedience to orders' as well.

That morning must have been an appalling occasion, no less so because it was common enough at that period. Three men each received 12 lashes. Four, including Jeffery, took 24 lashes and the eighth man, a marine, was given no less than 48. The bosun's mates, whose duty it was to wield the cat, must have exhausted themselves by the time they had inflicted the total of 180 lashes, even though the practice was for them to change over after each two dozen.

The following day the sloop anchored in Carlisle Bay, Barbados, and soon afterwards began a cruise, patrolling the Leeward Islands and the sea-passages between. One Saturday evening a fortnight or so later Jeffery succumbed again to temptation.[13]

The ship's water - according to Jeffery and some other witnesses - had run low which meant that the crew were rationed to a smaller allowance than usual. Feeling thirsty Jeffery went to a cask of spruce beer which was stowed

14

between decks and which 'belonged to the midshipman' (probably to the midshipmen's mess) where he drew off two quarts into a bucket. After drinking about three-quarters of it, he passed the rest to a sailor close by who had seen him.

Much later one of the crew said that what really had happened was that Jeffery, being armourer's mate, had lent one of his tools to some shipmates who used it to tap the beer cask.[14] If true, this both confirms that Jeffery was not the only one involved, but equally that (having access to a tool and having previously been found guilty of stealing liquor) he was an obvious suspect, particularly if he were correct in saying that the beer 'belonged to the midshipman', for it was one of the midshipmen who had reported the earlier offence which gained Jeffery a flogging. (The same witness adds the final irony that on the following day the beer was examined, found bad and thrown overboard.)

Was the *Recruit* really short of water? The master was to testify that on December 13 the brig had at least 17 tons of water on board. His log records that three tons of water were received as recently as November 27 on a second brief visit to Barbados.[15] A sloop with a crew of 135 usually carried 40 tons of water, and used it at the rate of half a ton a day.[16]

John Libby, one of the Polperro men, was to claim that the men were put on allowance 'so that the Officers had so much water as they pleased while the seamen had very little. He [presumably Libby himself] was often obliged to drink salt water & so were several of the seamen, some were ill with it'.[17] There seems no reason why the brig should have been seriously short of water, for she was never far from Barbados or other populated islands under British control. She had, in fact, travelled northward from Guiana to Barbados, continued her patrol past St Lucia, Guadeloupe, Puerto Rico and then cruised eastward near the Virgin Islands.)

Jeffery was reported by the very man who had shared the bucket of beer with him and was ordered to appear before the captain next morning, a Sunday. So it was probably following the usual divisions and inspection which preceded divine service when Captain Lake asked Jeffery if he had tapped the beer. Having admitted it he was then asked why he had done it. 'For being very hot, I was almost dying with thirst, and had been working hard all the day', was his reply. The captain ordered the marine serjeant to put his name on the black list of men to be given the unpleasant jobs to do, and sent him away. The lad and his shipmates must have thought he had got off remarkably lightly.

It was late on Sunday afternoon, December 13, 1807 two days after Jeffery's eighteenth birthday, that he was summoned again before the captain. [Jeffery himself claimed that a week had elapsed since his misdemeanour but the master and two seamen reported that the events occurred over a single weekend, that of December 12 and 13, which seems more likely.]

The ship was then in the Anegada passage, a wide sea lane east of the Virgin Islands and the main route from Europe to the West Indies. Mid-passage is the desolate, barren islet of Sombrero, so named by the Spaniards because of its resemblance in profile to a Spanish hat. Completely isolated, it lies 38 miles north of Anguilla and 55 miles east of Anegada in the British Virgin Islands. Some three-quarters of a mile long it is only 400 yards wide at its broadest point. Probably of volcanic origin, Sombrero has no beach, but is ringed instead by cliffs of eroded limestone, 20 to 40 feet high. Waterless and treeless, it was inhabited only by sea-birds and lizards.[18]

That Sunday afternoon, just before dusk, as the *Recruit* was passing a mile or so west of Sombrero, Captain Lake came on deck and asked the master, Edward Spencer, the island's name. 'Have we not some thieves on board?' he continued after being told. 'Two,' Spencer replied, one being Jeffery. The second was evidently a marine named Cornelius van Dam who was probably a serious offender, for he had been punished with six dozen lashes on 19 October.[19]

Lake ordered the marine serjeant to bring Jeffery from the

'tween-decks to the starboard gangway. The young man just had time to put on his smartest clothes - a blue jacket with mother-of-pearl buttons, and a white beaver hat. He was brought on deck, probably none too gently, and stood before the captain, waiting to hear why he had been suddenly called out.

His captain's words were so astounding that the few people who heard them could hardly have taken them seriously at first. Lake told the lad that 'he would not keep such a fellow in his ship', and that he intended to send him ashore on the island, now hazily visible about three-quarters of a mile to windward. According to one seaman who was present, he removed all doubt by telling Jeffery melodramatically that this was to be 'his doom': the boy would perish of thirst and hunger, for he was forbidden to take food, drink or extra clothes with him. Jeffery, thoroughly scared though hardly crediting this extraordinary threat, answered with tears in his eyes, 'I hope not, sir'.

The captain's response was to order the lad immediately to fetch up his clothes.[20] Lake ordered the ship's painter to get a piece of canvas, and paint on it 'Thief'. This was then sewn on to the back of the white frock which Jeffery was now wearing, having removed (perhaps been ordered to remove) his best blue jacket.

Lake, always a choleric man, by now had worked himself into a fury. The surgeon thought him demented; a seaman merely that he was 'rather in liquor', and the master that he was 'more passionate than usual'. He instructed the second lieutenant, Richard Mould, who was on deck about his duty, to take the jolly-boat to Sombrero, land Jeffery on the island, and return. The only reason he gave for this extraordinary order was that the lad had stolen some spruce beer.

Later it was suggested that the captain had been dining in the wardroom the evening before, when he was told of Jeffery's taking the beer.[21] Lake usually drank freely after dinner and, according to this version, it was then that he gave the order to put Jeffery ashore. The master, Spencer, for some reason taken a dislike to the boy, and remarked that it would be a good thing to get him off the ship as flogging would do him no good.[22] It may have been on this occasion that Spencer said as much to the captain, little expecting the remark to be taken seriously and acted upon.

In any case the order was not put into effect at that moment, no doubt because those who heard it hoped that when the captain sobered up he would have forgotten or changed his mind. Be that as it may, he was apparently in liquor now insisting that his order be obeyed.

While Lake was giving his instructions to Lieutenant Mould, some members of the crew close by told Jeffery there were 'some islands to the leeward of Sombrero', which he should make for, if he could get any timber with which to build a raft. No doubt the advice was kindly meant, but it was to prove impossible to take.[23]

Lieutenant Mould seems to have interceded with Lake on Jeffery's behalf, but the captain would have none of it. 'Speaking loudly and harshly', he ordered his steward to bring up his pistols, and had them laid on the capstan.

When Jeffery got back with his small bundle of clothing, Lake - like the bully he was - asked 'What have you got there?' The young man replied, 'My clothes, sir, which you ordered me to fetch'. The captain told him to drop them and get out of the ship. The jolly-boat was lowered, its crew commanded by Lieutenant Mould, supported by a midshipman named Salmond. Jeffery was ordered over the stern into the boat, wearing his white frock and trousers, and hat, but no shoes. The boat was hauled along the starboard side of the ship where Captain Lake still stood. Someone apparently pointed out that Jeffery's clothes had been left where the captain had told him to drop them, but Lake called down, 'Never mind his things', and ordered the boat's crew to shove off. As it was growing dark, Lake told Lieutenant Mould to make haste, land Jeffery and return on board.

When the boat reached the island ('the rock', Jeffery called it, which is really what Sombrero is), Mould followed by Midshipman Salmond scrambled ashore. They called Jeffery out, and he obeyed. One of the seamen in the boat, Francisco Valla, said that the boy was crying and through his sobs wished 'Good health' to 'the gentlemen and boat's crew.'[24]

Some of the boat's crew also went ashore, 'to see if there were any houses,' said Valla. The square outlines of the central rocks might be taken at a distance for houses; but of course the answer came back that there was none.

Jeffery had made his way up 'as high as the mizzen-top', Valla recalled. Having no shoes or stockings, the rugged, sharp rocks cut his feet which began to bleed profusely, whereupon he begged the lieutenant for shoes. Mould obtained a pair for him from one of the boat's crew on the lieutenant's promise that they would be replaced once back on board. Another shipmate passed a knife to Jeffery, thinking it might be useful when he had to fend for himself. Both the officers gave him handkerchiefs which he might wave to attract the attention of a passing ship if one happened to come close enough.[25]

Up to that point Jeffery must have had some faint hope that this was all unreal, some sort of cruel charade to frighten him. Now, as it grew darker and the officers prepared to leave the boat, it slowly dawned on him that he was to be left alone on the rock, at least for the night. He pleaded to the lieutenant 'In the name of God, sir, what am I to do?' The enormity of the situation had perhaps only just struck Mould himself. He clasped the boy by the hand (Jeffery afterwards said the officer was shedding tears as he did so, though that may have been hindsight's imagination). All the advice the lieutenant could offer was that Jeffery should 'keep a sharp look-out for ships that pass'. As if he would fail to do that, knowing there was no certainty that a ship would pass close enough to notice him before he died of starvation, thirst or exposure.

The boy, weeping, begged one of the boat's crew to tell Libby - a Polperro man, who must have known the family - not to let his mother know what had happened to him.[26]

Within fifteen minutes of landing, Lieutenant Mould climbed down to the shore, no doubt preceded by the midshipman, boarded the boat, and ordered the crew to shove off. He last saw Robert Jeffery on the shore, his hands raised in entreaty 'appearing in the most dreadful agony of spirit'.[27]

Jeffery stood with hands clasped, tears rolling down his cheeks, as he watched the boat approach the brig. As night fell and he could see the ship no longer, he threw himself down despairingly on the ground, and stayed like that most of the night.

When morning came - Monday, December 14 - he looked across to the *Recruit* only to see her under sail and already moving. Clutching at any slight hope, he thought she might come in closer to Sombrero and, his nightmare ordeal over, send a boat to pick him up. But it soon became clear that nothing of the kind would happen. The *Recruit* was moving away to the south. First hull, then masts, disappeared over the horizon.

Robert Jeffery, the 18-year-old Cornish lad who had sought adventure at sea, was quite alone, under the tropical sun, on a bare, desolate rock almost 40 miles from the nearest inhabited land.

Chapter 2

THE ADMIRAL'S BLIND EYE

The crew were in no doubt of what had been done to their shipmate, for all hands had been on deck when the boat was lowered. Whatever some of the officers thought or hoped, the lower-deck did not imagine Sombrero to be anything but what it was, an uninhabited, bare patch of rock. The serjeant of marines heard them muttering among themselves that the boy would starve to death, and heard the master come up behind them and say 'You be damned'.[1]

It was between seven and eight pm when the boat got back to the *Recruit* after landing young Jeffery. As Lieutenant Mould came over the gangway he was heard to remark that the island was a barren, uninhabited, place. Neither he nor anyone else seems to have dared to make such a remark in the hearing of the captain.

Next morning the ship was still in sight of Sombrero, which lay about south-west by west of the vessel, 15 to 18 miles away. At that distance, even if any officer had troubled to use a glass, he could not possibly have seen poor Jeffery trying to attract attention in the hope of being taken back aboard. But it was not too far, or too late, for rescue. Lieutenant Mould had the morning watch, four to eight am, and was followed by the master, Edward Spencer. Between eight and nine Captain Lake came on deck. There is a suggestion that one officer or another pointed out the island to him, with the implication that it was still possible to turn back and send a boat for Jeffery, but if so there was no response.[2] The ship continued on her course, and the island soon disappeared astern.

That evening Spencer dined with the captain. As Lake got up from the table he said: 'I wonder how old friend Jeffery comes on now; I suppose he is got housed by this time'. Unless he was being sarcastically cruel, he must have convinced himself, perhaps through a blur of liquor, that the island really was inhabited. A glance at one of the current gazetteers[3] would have informed him that it was not, even if he had cared nothing for the opinion of Lieutenant Mould who had actually been ashore there. But it was unlikely that they possessed one. Spencer, although he was sailing master, did not even have an instruction book for navigating in the West Indies. 'But I have seen one,' he told the eventual court martial. (He would have had to purchase his own: the Admiralty did not go in for free issues.)

However, a court martial was to be far in the future. No one, not even the captain, seems to have thought on those lines yet. The *Recruit* went about her duties, patrolling the Caribbean, where one island - Guadeloupe - was still held by the French, and enemy privateers could still operate.

Robert Jeffery's clothes, which he had been ordered to leave behind, were served out to members of the crew by the captain's order: probably sold to them, as when a seaman died. When anyone offended Lake he was now apt to say that, 'he knew other uninhabited islands, besides Sombrero'.[4] The fate of young Jeffery must have remained a topic of conversation, on the lower deck at least, for long afterwards. Opinions no doubt varied as to whether he had died from thirst and hunger, or been attacked by the swarms of sea-birds, whether he had managed to make some kind of raft and reached another island or been picked up; or whether he had been seen by a passing ship and rescued, perhaps quite quickly. Among the most concerned about his fate were probably his shipmates from Polperro, Libby and Richard Johns; and Lieutenant Mould, himself a Fowey man, seems to have retained some sort of compassion while not daring to cross Lake. In January the carpenter was confined to his cabin for insolence to the captain, perhaps a reflection of the general opinion of Lake's heartless attitude over the Jeffery incident.[5]

For the captain and the officers, whatever their view of what had occurred, there was one small problem to be attended to. How was the abandonment of a seaman upon a desert island to be entered in the ship's books? In HMS *Recruit*, as in other naval vessels, four sets of books were kept: captain's log, master's log, first lieutenant's log and the muster books.

The basic navigational information - course, wind direction and so on - was entered on a slate by each officer of the watch. It was then copied by (or for) the captain, the master and the first lieutenant respectively into the draft log required to be kept by each of them. Finally, a fair copy was made of each for submission to the Admiralty. In most cases the captain's and the master's logs have been preserved and can be seen today at The National Archives in Kew. Not so many lieutenants' logs survive, and those which do are in the National Maritime Museum, Greenwich. In the case of HMS *Recruit*, all three logs (captain's, master's and lieutenant's) survive for the period which interests us. It must be remembered, however, that in each case the book we now see is the fair copy, the third of three stages.

First, the log kept by Lake himself.[6] He did not record punishments in his log and in his entry for Sunday, December 13, 1807 he made no reference to the Jeffery incident at all. For the significant evening he recorded, 'At 6, Fresh Breezes. Sombrero N.W. Tacked Occasionally to Weather the Island. At 7 the Island SSW 3 Leagues. At 7.30 Squally. Split the Jib, unbent ditto and bent another'.

One wonders what went through Lake's mind when he wrote up his log that weekend, or approved what was written for him. However strong his contempt for the lad whom he thought dishonest, a weakling and of no consequence, he cannot have expected to avoid accounting at some stage for him. Not that the loss of a man was unusual, what with deaths through accident or disease, and frequent desertion; but something had to be recorded. It seems likely that Lake thought the incident could be explained away, or brazened out somehow, at a later stage by simply 'discharging' Jeffery at Sombrero. The authorities, not knowing the island, might conceivably have swallowed such a story, and the discharge of a seaman did not have to be recorded in the log-book.

Edward Spencer, master of the *Recruit*, left the master's mate, a young man named George Jones, to write up his log 'under his direction', as he claimed later. From time to time he checked the entries. Whether or not Jones (who as master's mate, was a potential commissioned officer, the equivalent of a sub-lieutenant) was frightened to record the Sombrero incident, he certainly did not (according to Spencer) do so. If Spencer can be believed, he himself discovered the omission several days later, and inserted the sentence, 'lowered down boat and landed Robert Jeffery, seaman, 6.50, up boat, and made sail'.[7]

This is what Spencer told the court martial, much later, and the minutes show that a log-book was handed to him and identified. The words said to have been inserted were read out by Spencer. He stated that Lake was unaware that this entry had been inserted (presumably no one would dare tell him), but the officers did know. Jones, who had omitted the item in the first place, died of fever on May 22, 1808, and so could not be questioned at the court martial. In fact Spencer's log gives the same navigational material as that of the captain, but after 'weathered the island' there follow simply the words, 'lowered a Boat down & landed Robt Jefferys seaman on the Island of Sombrero'[8] - a slight but curious divergence from the wording read in court, as it contains no reference to the return of the boat and making sail.

This 'insertion' is in the same handwriting as the rest of the log, to be expected if the change were made at the rough draft stage. But in that case, and if the man who wrote the draft were dead, why did Spencer have to refer to it at all? Even more oddly, an Irish seaman named Peter Bowen in a letter written to the Admiralty after the court martial referred to 'me at the Same time Keeping Mr Spencer the Masters Log & Journal'.[9] Did the master's mate, Jones, further depute the job to a young seaman whom he knew to be literate?

Lastly we may look at the log kept by Lieutenant Higgins, the first lieutenant, who apparently played no part in the drama. His version lies somewhere between the two others: 'Hove too [sic] and landed Robt Jefferys on the Island. at 7 the Island SSW, 3 Leagues. 7.30 Squally W. Split the Jib.'[10]

There remained the muster book, which had to go to the Navy Board as evidence of entitlement to pay.[11] This was kept by the acting purser, James Hobson. He, too, was probably at a loss how to describe the departure of Jeffery and equally must have hesitated to consult the captain. Had he decided to put a 'D' for 'discharged', it might have passed unnoticed. Instead, he settled for 'R' for 'run' - deserted: which would have caused raised eyebrows to anyone who got wind of the true story.

When Hobson was questioned at the court martial, he admitted knowing what had actually occurred, but said he believed he had entered 'R' of his own accord.[12] Long after the incident, and only six weeks before the court martial (that is, in December, 1809, when a naval inquiry was already on foot), Lake personally asked Hobson what the muster-book showed. According to Hobson, the captain then told him he should have entered Jeffery as having been discharged, and he should now take out the 'R' and make an entry of his being discharged to Sombrero. Hobson did not do so, he later told the court, because he believed he had already sent up an earlier muster book in which the 'R' had been entered. Lake had signed that earlier book, but had apparently not noticed the entry.

The muster-books, like the logs, can be seen today at The National Archives; each covers a period of two months, but a man remained on the list until the crew were paid off. In the earliest relevant book, covering December 13, the day Jeffery was put ashore, the entry against his name has been scratched out. Only the word 'Sombrero' can be faintly made out. Each succeeding book shows 'R', 'Sombrero Island', and the date, December 13, 1807. A book was produced at the court martial, showing the 'R' entry.

After the court martial, by which time this matter was almost academic, the Navy Board reported to the Admiralty on the musterbooks.[13] They pointed out that in the muster book for November and December, 1807 Jeffery was 'not Mustered the 20th and 27th December but pricked without leave, thus: Sombrero Islands 14 December; and on the next Book for January and February, 1808 he is noted Run 13th Decr 1807 Sombrero Island.'.

A man was not normally marked as 'run' until he had missed three successive musters; if he returned before then, he was regarded only as a 'straggler' and did not receive the severe punishment for desertion. Which book did the court martial see: the earlier one or the later one? And why and when was the earlier one tampered with? The answer to the latter question proved to be less mysterious than appeared. When the Navy Board reported, in April 1810, the 'R' was still to be seen in the earlier book; but among the court martial papers is a rough note that the Board was ordered to remove the 'Run' entry. The crude scratching out of the entry in the earlier book is presumably in execution of this order; perhaps the clerk simply did not trouble with the later ones.

Christmas came and went, and the *Recruit* continued her cruise southward. Eventually on January 29, 1808 she anchored again in Carlisle Bay, Barbados. Rear-Admiral Sir Alexander Cochrane was there already, in his flagship HMS *Dart*. The Sombrero incident must still have been the talk of the lower-deck in the *Recruit*. Although shore-leave was virtually non-existent in the wartime navy, there must have been many informal contacts with other ships as boats' crews ferried officers to and from the flagship or the quayside, and seamen were detached to take prize vessels into port.

It was hardly surprising, therefore, that word of the affair quickly reached the admiral, Sir Alexander Cochrane, a 50-year-old Scot who was, like Warwick Lake, a younger son. His father was the eighth Earl of Dundonald, and his elder brother Archibald, after beginning his career in the navy, had become an eminent scientist. Archibald's son, Thomas, was to become Admiral Sir Thomas Cochrane (1775-1860), one of the greatest naval commanders in history, who played a leading part not only in the British navy, but in the fleets of Chile, Peru, Brazil and Greece in the liberation of those countries.

Although Sir Alexander was to be outshone by his nephew, he was an able enough officer. He won steady wartime promotion, and had been a rear-admiral since 1804. From 1800 to 1806 he also held a seat in Parliament (for the Stirling boroughs). More interesting, in the light of future events, is the fact that his nephew Thomas Cochrane was elected to Parliament for Westminster in 1807 with Sir Francis Burdett, both being radical reformers and campaigners against abuses in the navy.

Sir Alexander was now told that one of his commanders, a member of an important and influential family, in what appeared to be a fit of drunken fury had landed one of his seamen on a desolate tropical island and left him there. If that were not a potential naval scandal, what was? No doubt the admiral sent for Lake, but what passed at such an interview we can only guess. It must have been evident from the outset that the report was true, no matter how Lake tried to justify his action. What was to be done?

Cochrane's main task after all was to fight a continuing, if diminishing, war in the West Indies. Whatever the reforming views of his young nephew Thomas, Sir Alexander was a man of his generation, who accepted many abuses in the navy and was not above taking part himself. When a young captain he had, unknown to his brother Archibald, entered his nephew Thomas from the age of five in the books of various ships under his command, with the idea that when the boy became old enough actually to go to sea (which he did not do until rather late, when he was 18) he would already have a few years' standing in the Service.[14] In fact another relative with military influence obtained a commission in the army for Thomas, so in theory while still a schoolboy he was in both services at the same time!

Such false musters derived from nepotism and greed, and only marginally concerned human rights, of which the British naval seaman enjoyed few at the best of times. Leaving a man to his fate on an uninhabited island was going far too far, and if nephew Thomas heard of it there might be the devil to pay. However, England and Parliament were leagues away and communications were slow. If Jeffery were still on the island, and could be returned to his ship, perhaps the whole matter might be forgotten? A court martial would bring it all into the open, and would not help the luckless castaway. So the admiral decided to treat the episode as a minor abuse of power by one of his junior commanders. 'I was well aware of the irregularity of the proceeding' was the strongest expression he chose to describe his reaction in a letter to the Admiralty much later.[15] In a man who had himself been an MP it was a curiously insensitive attitude.

The only action he took at this stage was to send Captain Lake back to the island in the *Recruit* to find Jeffery, and take him on board again. Lake, of all people, was the one chosen to 'rescue' the man. What reception could Jeffery expect from this particular rescuer? But, of course, the whole idea was to keep the matter from going further if at all possible.

So on February 1 the *Recruit* weighed anchor and sailed back to Sombrero. By the time she arrived there it was February 11, two months after Jeffery had been marooned. Lake sent Spencer and Lieutenant Mould ashore that morning to locate Jeffery, or at least to determine what sort of island it was. In his court martial evidence later Spencer described what they discovered.[16]

One thing was certain: they found neither Jeffery nor his remains.

It was now the breeding season for the Noddy terns which nested on Sombrero, and the search party came upon a great many eggs, and young birds still in the nest. They found no fresh water; every pool which Spencer tasted was salt. The island was entirely barren, except for 'a kind of rough grass weed' in the middle of the island. There were no houses, no inhabitants.

Spencer said he surveyed minutely every part of the island, which had a craggy ascent, was flat at the top and measured about a mile and a half in circumference. After an hour and a half the searchers returned on board at midday. That afternoon they made a further trip, this time accompanied by Hobson, the purser, and Salmond, a midshipman. They surveyed the island, taking different routes. Still no trace of Jeffery, though they did come across a remnant of a pair of trousers, much torn. The handle of a tomahawk or hatchet was the only other evidence that any human being had visited the island. On this second trip they felt their time might be turned to advantage, so they brought muskets and slugs to shoot birds. At about six or seven in the evening they brought back with them some of the eggs and young birds. Lake himself came to the shore of the island, but did not land and returned to the ship with the search party.

Back in Barbados on February 17, Lake found - or so he said later - a statement in an American newspaper that Jeffery had been taken off the island and landed in America. In the light of later events, it was unfortunate that no one kept a copy of this newspaper report (assuming it did exist) or even a note of the date and the name of the paper.

In any case both Lake and Cochrane seem to have convinced themselves that because no trace of Jeffery had been found, the lad must have been rescued and was now safe. Had he died on the rock, they no doubt reasoned, at least his skeleton would have been discovered. Any other fate, such as drowning, which might have overtaken him must be mere speculation and need not be considered. The captain and the admiral must have hoped that the problem, like Jeffery, would simply disappear.

When Admiral Cochrane was told of the American newspaper report, he 'consented, after seriously admonishing Captain Lake, to let the business rest'.[17] Lake himself was

29

heard by Hobson, acting purser, to say 'he was very sorry it had happened, he would rather have given £20,000'.[18] This, said Hobson, 'was after he had been to the Admiral, at Barbadoes'.

It must have been about this time that Warwick Lake received the news that his father, the celebrated General Viscount Lake, had died in February. The new viscount was Warwick's elder brother Francis Gerard, gazetted the same year as lieutenant colonel of the 60th.

In June (1808) Warwick Lake was sent home on sick leave. With hindsight we may question, as others did, whether he was really sick, or sent home in disgrace, or for family reasons, or just to get him off the station. As if to guard against such doubts, the admiral went through a remarkably elaborate procedure. A court of inquiry, composed as usual of three captains, assembled on board HMS *York* in Carlisle Bay, Barbados on June 13, 1808 - seven months to the day since poor Jeffery was left on Sombrero.[19] They were assisted by the physician inspector, and the surgeons of the three ships commanded by the captains: the *York* (Captain W. Barton), the *Captain* (Captain J. S. Wolley) and the *Belleisle* (Captain W. Manor). Presumably they called in Lake and questioned him, but no one else from the *Recruit* is mentioned as being present.

This imposing body certified that 'we find him subject to frequent attacks of Vomitting, that he labours under a loss of appetite and general debility; we therefore recommend a Change of Climate, as absolutely necessary for the recovery of his health'. On the face of it, this diagnosis of Lake seems to indicate little more than heavy drinking combined with the effect of the climate (and just possibly worry, if not remorse, over the Sombrero incident). It was one thing to be granted leave, another to get home so it was some time before Lake was found a passage, in HMS *Camilla*, to England, where he landed on August 13.[20] He put up at Blake's Hotel in Jermyn Street, and reported his arrival to the Admiralty. It may or may not be significant that aparently he did not go straight

30

to his brother's house. That same month another of the Lake brothers was killed at the battle of Vimiero, in Portugal.

Warwick Lake can have only just have heard this further piece of bad news when, in mid-September, he was ordered by the Admiralty to go back to the West Indies and resume command of the *Recruit*.[21] Before he left he may have been told one encouraging thing: the Admiralty (who still knew nothing of the Sombrero incident) was sending a blank commission to Admiral Cochrane to make him post-captain at the first vacancy.[22]

Writing again from Blake's Hotel, Jermyn Street, after only a month's leave, he asked for a passage out, and was told to travel to Plymouth and sail in the *Neptune*; in the event this seems to have been altered to *Intrepid*. When he reached the West Indies he received his appointment as post-captain, in command of HMS *Ulysses*.[23]

The man who had relieved him as commander of the *Recruit* was Charles (later Admiral Sir Charles) Napier. Under this gallant sailor, the *Recruit* earned a more creditable place in naval history. On September 6, while Lake was still in England, Napier had fought a spirited action with the French sloop *Diligente*. Although his thigh was broken, he refused to leave the deck until the fall of the *Recruit*'s mainmast ended the engagement. In February 1809 he distinguished himself at the taking of Martinique, and two months after that he engaged and captured a 74-gun French ship, many times the size of the little English brig. Cochrane took the French vessel into the Royal Navy and appointed Napier as her captain. None of these things might have happened had Lake's original instructions to resume command of the *Recruit* taken effect.

When Lake had left HMS *Recruit*, Lieutenant Mould was ordered to another ship (the *Nimrod*).[24] Midshipman Graham, who was reponsible for Jeffery's getting a flogging for stealing beer, was sent home with Lake. James Hobson, the acting purser (we shall meet him again), had been transferred ten days earlier to a similar position in the sloop *Demerary*.[25]

Lieutenant Higgins, the first lieutenant, remained in the *Recruit* for another three months and Edward Spencer, the master, stayed on also.[26]

Including Robert Jeffery, ten men had been pressed from the *Lord Nelson* privateer on that August day at Falmouth, the year before. All save one were still serving in *Recruit* on the day when Jeffery was landed on Sombrero.[27] (John Johns, a 40-year-old Polperro man, had been discharged from the navy before the ship left Falmouth, perhaps because he was found to have had a valid protection or was considered unfit.)

The Plymouth man William Hitchens, who was 42, actually gained promotion on December 1, being made captain of the fo'csle; nevertheless he took an opportunity to desert in February, 1808 at Barbados when he was lent for service in a schooner. Two of the Scandinavians, Brown and Isaacson, also deserted in the West Indies. William May, from Plymouth, was discharged to another ship on June 25 and paid off, no doubt being given passage home.

John Libby and young Richard Johns, the two remaining Polperro men, were sent to England in *Camilla,* with Captain Lake, Midshipman Graham, and two others from *Recruit.* On arrival at Sheerness, Libby and Johns were discharged from the Service.[28] Of the original *Lord Nelson* ten, only the Irishman William Kelly was then left aboard the *Recruit.*

Not only had Lake, Mould, Graham and Hobson been sent away from the ship, but Jeffery's two friends from Polperro had also been removed. However, it would not have required much imagination to foresee Libby and Johns spreading the news of Jeffery's fate at home. If, when they got back to Cornwall, they did tell the story (and after all Jeffery had asked them not to let his mother know) no protest seems to have been made. Even Jeffery's parents, who were later to become vocal enough, may - if they knew the story - have assumed the lad to be dead and that to confront the authorities now would be useless. When eventually Libby and Johns were

Robert Jeffery: engraving after E M Jones, 1811
National Portrait Gallery, London

Robert Jeffery: fictitious portrait engraving published by
C. Chrippes, 1810
National Portrait Gallery, London

HMS *Recruit* under attack by a French '74, in 1809
National Maritime Museum

Extract from the *Recruit*'s log book *National Archives*

Typical Marblehead schooner, the *Raven*, when Ambrose
Martin was her master
Marblehead Historical Society

VIEW OF THE TOWN OF MARBLEHEAD, MASSACHUSETTS.

Marblehead, Massachusetts, in the mid-19th century
Peabody Museum, Salem

questioned by the authorities, the episode was already public knowledge.

And if by some miracle the lad were still alive, where was he and why had no one heard from him?

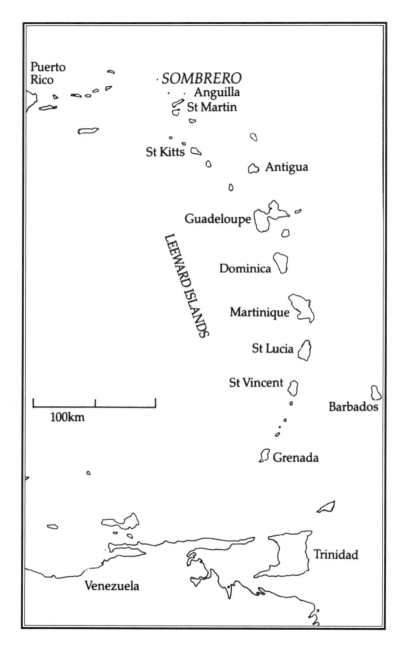

Puerto
Rico

·SOMBRERO

· · Anguilla

St Martin

St Kitts

Antigua

Guadeloupe

LEEWARD ISLANDS

Dominica

Martinique

St Lucia

St Vincent

Barbados

100km

Grenada

Trinidad

Venezuela

[from the orginal by Iris Derriman]

Chapter 3

'THE GOVERNOR OF SOMBRERO'

We left Robert Jeffery alone on his desolate island, weeping in despair as he saw the *Recruit* disappear over the horizon.

In a story where there is almost too much contemporary documentation, one passage in particular deserves to be quoted in full. It is Jeffery's own account of his ordeal on the island, dictated much later, but set out day by day, with the ring of truth.[1] More than one version of it was published, beginning - as we shall see - with a statement made under oath. Although the order and timing of the details vary, allowance must be made for memory becoming a little blurred in the three years or so before the story was put down on paper. The essential points remain unchanged, and in the later version mistakes made in the earlier ones may well have been corrected by the 'author'.

> *First night* I then, with trembling steps, took a view of my unfortunate situation, threw myself down full of grief, and remained in that state the greatest part of the night.

> *First day* Day coming on, I saw, as I supposed, the brig bearing towards the rock, but soon was aware she took another course. I then traversed the rock, in hopes of seeing some other ship pass; but those I saw were at too great a distance for me to hail them. Being greatly exhausted, and my lips parched with the excessive heat of a West India sun, I was obliged to drink of the salt

water, which was the only nourishment I was able to find. I then threw myself down on my bed of flint, and endeavoured to take some repose; but sleep was not left for me.

Second night Night coming on, I became more resigned to my unhappy fate, being in hopes that Providence would release me the next day, and with little or no sleep, *prayer* was my only resource.

Second day At the dawn of this day, I went out in search of food; but could not find any, not even a blade of grass, a weed, or a limpet. It has been reported that I had limpets, but this is without foundation; every body who has seen the rock, well knows that there are none there, nor any other article which could possibly be converted into food. Hunger became more violent; but there was no other resource but the salt water, which made me worse.

Third night Part of the third night I spent in *prayers*, and at day-break of the

Third day I again traversed the rock, in search of food, and found an egg, but could not eat it, as it was in a very putrid state: it being out of season for birds to lay. It rained on this day, which enabled me to get a little fresh water. Hunger became more violent; and rendered me restless the whole of this day, and during the

Fourth night My distress no tongue can describe.

Fourth day I wandered about, searching every crevice of the rock: saw a small piece of the *bark of a tree*, about the size of a man's hand, which had been washed on the rock by the sea. I looked at it as if astonished at the great blessing, took it up, and eat [sic] it as if it had been the greatest luxury. Notwithstanding the sun had dried up all its moisture, still, it in some measure satisfied nature, and hunger now for a time, left me.

Fifth night Night drawing on, I again laid me down to sleep; but was continually alarmed by what had troubled me before, *black lizards crawling over my face*, and being ignorant of the harmlessness of those creatures, I remained restless *the whole* of that night'.

Fifth day Thirst became more violent than before. I now found the value of my shipmate's last gift, which was the knife before mentioned. With this I cut *the quills* from the feathers which were shed from the sea-birds, (some of which are called boobies,) which visit the rock, and by the assistance of these, I was enabled to suck *the rain-water from the crevices*, which was not to be got at any other way'.

Sixth night The refreshment I got from the rain enabled me to take some little repose.

Sixth day I was refreshed by more showers of rain, and supplied with a little more fresh water. I saw two vessels pass at a great distance.

Seventh night On this night, the heavens were as light as noon-day, arising from a continuation of strong flashes of lightning, which were followed by violent claps of thunder. The awfulness of this night was beyond description. Think what must have been my feelings to be without food, without cloathing, and even without a human being to sympathise with me in my sufferings. I gave myself up to despair, and earnestly prayed God to release me from misery.

Seventh day On this day in the morning, a ship hove in sight, which gave me fresh hopes; but they were soon banished by her steering another course, when she soon disappeared. I found myself now more forlorn, more miserable, and more hopeless than ever. Overcome with weakness, and being nearly exhausted, I became more resigned to my fate, and ended the lingering day in prayers.

Eighth night Heavy dews and very cold, but no hole nor cavern to creep into; yet on the

Eighth day The rock was so hot by the heat of the sun, that it was almost insupportable. I stripped myself of my jacket and trousers, and bathed myself in the puddles of salt water which lodged in parts of the rock, and which were thrown there by sprays of the sea. This I had done before, and it relieved me much, and I laid me down and had some repose.

Ninth night Was not so cold as some of the preceding nights, which enabled me to sleep the greater part of it. Providence must have ordained it to enable my strength to support me in the exertions I used in hailing the schooner *Adams*, Captain John Dennis, from Martinique, bound for Marblehead in America. This was the WELCOME VESSEL, that on the *ninth day*, at half past two in the afternoon, released me from my sufferings!!

As soon as the light returned the next morning, worn out as I was, yet being still on the alert, I was in a transport of joy, and felt as if I knew she was coming to release me from my horrible situation. Raised with hope, and yet distressed with the anxiety of making myself seen, I walked to and fro, waving my hat, for I had done the same in vain on several former occasions.

The captain, *John Dennis*, had no business near the rock, and therefore PROVIDENCE must have led him under the force of curiosity, to turn out of his course, and lay to all night; for he afterwards told me that he had determined the preceding night to view it the first thing in the morning, through his telescope.

While he was thus reconnoitring the rock, he indistinctly perceived *me* waving my hat, as well as a number of birds, which were hovering about the rock.

From the motion of the vessel, and the doubtful light of the morning, which was not far advanced, he supposed me, as he seriously affirmed, to be of the *feathered tribe*, though of an enormous size; but upon laying closer in, and the light increasing, the mate, Joseph Dickson, got up in the shrouds, and soon discovered me to be a HUMAN BEING!

The schooner lowered its boat and, said Jeffery, the crew vied with each other to go to the rescue. Not unnaturally they supposed that the young man must have been shipwrecked. He was so exhausted that when they reached the island he rolled into the arms of the mate, and was helped into the boat. It was now December 22, nine days since Jeffery had been left on Sombrero.

On board the 63-ton *Adams*[2], the captain and his crew gathered round to express their sympathy for the 'shipwrecked' youngster. When he told them he had been put on the rock by his captain 'for taking about a couple of quarts of spruce beer', and of his ordeal there, they were speechless for a moment. Then they unhesitatingly spoke their minds, and hoped that the captain might meet the same punishment for his cruelty.

They gave Jeffery the best of what they had, and he drank a little wine and water, made warm; but he had been without nourishment so long that he could not keep it down. Someone then remembered that the captain had three or four days' supply of oranges, lately taken on board. These did the trick, and the young man soon regained his appetite. 'In little more than a week, I was able to eat more than any one man in the ship, and my strength increased a little daily.'

The schooner was on the homeward leg of what was evidently one of the normal voyages of the Marblehead fleet: outward to the West Indies with dried fish, homeward to Massachusetts with sugar. This time - it was, of course, midwinter - the *Adams* met bad weather, and took five weeks to reach her home port, probably twice as long as usual. By the time they arrived, Robert Jeffery had nearly recovered.

Of all places in America for a Cornishman to find himself, Marblehead must have seemed a home from home. Indeed the founders of this seaport, on the Massachusetts coast 14 miles north-east of Boston, had included fishermen from Cornwall. One of the early leaders of the community, Hugh Peters, had been a minister from Fowey, whose mother was a Treffry.[3]

Marblehead is built on a rocky peninsula on one side of a natural harbour, across which it faces the town of Salem. When Jeffery landed there towards the end of January, 1808 fishing was still its people's main livelihood, just as it was at Polperro. At Marblehead, bigger even than Fowey, however, it was cod, not pilchards which were salted and dried for export to the West Indies in schooners like the *Adams*, and exchanged for sugar to be taken to Boston for making into rum and molasses. In winter the cottagers turned to shoe-making which developed into a flourishing industry, later to move elsewhere. Today, the magnificent harbour of Marblehead has resulted in its becoming 'the yachting capital of America'.

Nevertheless, a modern description of the town is remarkably reminiscent of - say - Fowey, 'Marblehead, in whose narrow, twisted streets traditions linger, is built upon a rock, and everywhere through their garment of turf protrude knobs and cliffs of granite. Along the steep, winding ways weather-beaten houses shoulder each other, with intermittent glimpses of the harbor and the sea between their grayed walls. A mass of tumbled rocks chiseled by the sea forms the grim profile of the Neck'.[4]

The people of Marblehead were no lovers of the British. The town had been prosperous until the Boston tea party when it became a centre of rebel patriotism - and impoverished. It is still proud of being 'the birthplace of the American Navy' because General Washington commissioned the first American warship in 1775, owned and manned by Marblehead men. After the war, with many of its menfolk killed and the few loyalists driven out, the community returned to fishing.

Although the port had slowly recovered its prosperity the schooner *Adams*, with Robert Jeffery on board, returned to a Marblehead again on the brink of depression. In December, 1807 while the *Adams* had been away in the West Indies, Congress had passed the Embargo Act which closed all American ports to foreign trade in an attempt to bring both the British and French to terms. Captain Dennis found that the schooner had been making her last (at least, her last legal) voyage to the West Indies for the indefinite future. In fact the embargo was eventually repealed in the following year, 1809, as a result of its disastrous effect on the American economy.

So far as young Robert Jeffery was concerned, this situation had two immediate effects: if he wished to return to Britain, or even send a letter to tell his family that he was safe, there was no vessel to take him or it.

When the schooner reached Marblehead, the kindly mate, Joseph Dickson, took Robert into his own house and let the young man live there for nearly three weeks, until he was able to work. Meanwhile Dickson went round the townsfolk collecting a subscription for him. Some contributed clothes, of which he was urgently in need, for this was a New England winter, and others money. By now it was February, and back in the West Indies the *Recruit* had just returned to Sombrero, and found Jeffery gone.

A local butcher named John Wayman needed a servant so Jeffery, still too weak to find work in a smithy, gladly took on the job for the next three weeks in exchange for his food and drink. Then he managed to find employment with a blacksmith, Israel Martin, in Beverly, some five miles away to the north of Salem Habour.[5] In this old agricultural, commercial and industrial town, there would have been plenty of work for a smith. He stayed with Martin for the next two months, at eight dollars a month plus free board and lodging, hardly a princely wage, but it was a start.

Jeffery next moved to Hamilton, a village in attractive countryside some six miles further north, where he was employed for three months by a blacksmith named David Dodge. This time the pay was nine dollars a month plus board and lodging. By then Captain Lake was on his way back to England, on sick leave. Jeffery's next job - whether his frequent moves were from choice or necessity we do not know - was at the pleasant small town of Ipswich close by, near the mouth of the river of that name. There he worked for five months with a blacksmith named Amos Jones at ten dollars a month.

Then he returned to Hamilton and went to work for a farmer, John Adams, as a labourer. It must once more have been winter, which seems a curious time to find an agricultural job, but we are dependent for these details on what Jeffery remembered some time later.

As he recalled it, he then moved a few miles south again, to a farming hamlet named Wenham, between Hamilton and Beverly, nestling in a dell by a large lake. A small conical hill (since levelled) near the lake was the scene of the first sermon preached in the New World by Hugh Peters of Fowey, as Jeffery may well have been told. At Wenham, in the summer of 1809, 18 months after the Sombrero incident, he was taken on by another blacksmith, Ziell Dodge, again at ten dollars a month.

Robert Jeffery seems to have settled down happily enough, and was still at Wenham a year later. He made no secret of his story, and many people in and around Marblehead came to know it. He was even given a friendly nickname - 'the Governor of Sombrero'.

Partly as a result of the Embargo Act which had prevented foreign shipping, no one in authority in England had yet the least idea of what had happened or where he was. But that was soon to change.

Chapter 4

A PECULIAR PURSER

When the story that a seaman had been marooned by his captain on a desert island eventually reached the Admiralty, it was from an odd source and one which inspired little confidence.

Charles Morgan Thomas was a young man from Bristol, whose name and talent for emotional self-expression suggest a family origin on the other side of the Bristol Channel. Three years previously, early in 1806, Thomas had been found by Cochrane's secretary wandering in the streets of Barbados, penniless and friendless.[1] How he came to be in the West Indies, and what was the cause of his misfortune, are a mystery. Thomas begged to be given some kind of employment to keep him from starving, and the captain of the flagship put him to work in the office there. This is how the episode was told by the admiral, and although Thomas later quibbled about details, there is no reason to doubt its essential truth.

On one small point, however, there is a discrepancy. In a letter written in 1810 Thomas implied that he had served under Admiral Cochrane at the battle of St Domingo (February 6, 1806) and been wounded there. If so, his subsequent conduct might be explained by his having suffered mentally as well as physically. However, this explanation is hardly consistent with Cochrane's statement to his secretary that Thomas was 'an utter stranger'. Any sensible secretary would surely have become aware that the man had recently been discharged wounded or had deserted, if either were true. Moreover, the date of his appointment as clerk in the secretary's office on the flagship was dated February 18, 1806 - only 12 days after the battle.[2]

At first Charles Thomas seems to have worked satisfactorily, and within the year his charm won him an appointment as acting purser in a small sloop, HMS *Heureux*. It soon became clear that as well as having a way with words, he was thoroughly unbalanced, a self-centred and quarrelsome character. He began to develop a persecution mania.

He made accusations against the captain of *Heureux*, which the admiral took seriously enough to order an inquiry by three captains who found the charges frivolous and groundless. At his own request, Thomas was then allowed on July 8, 1808 to exchange posts with the (acting) purser of another, smaller sloop, the *Demerary*. And by some odd coincidence the man with whom he exchanged was James Hobson, who had left the *Recruit* on June 14, at the same time as Captain Lake.

Hobson probably got the better of the bargain. The *Demerary* had been bought second-hand and was in poor shape. The officers, Thomas wrote later, had no cabins, but 'small sleeping bed-places', and the purser (himself) had not even that. Often he had to get out of his cot at night because the rain was 'running thro' her decks like a riddle, nay thro' her very beams'.[3]

Neither of Thomas's appointments was confirmed by the Admiralty. He could not agree with any of the captains with whom he served, and was continually pestering Admiral Cochrane with letters of complaint which grew wilder as time went on. News of some kind of family misfortune seems to have pushed him over the edge of rational conduct. In January 1809, still in the *Demerary*, he was threatening the admiral that 'if more provoked' he would disclose facts which would involve 'if not all, at least the greater part of the Captains of the Squadron under your command'. He would give his information in the first instance to Government ministers, and if they took no notice he would 'take a walk to St Stephens Chappel' (the House of Commons) 'and report it there.'

He added (with a foresight remarkable in a man who had been exiled in the West Indies for some years), 'I already anticipate the remarks that will appear in Cobbett's *Register*'. He himself would make his own comments in the Barbados *Mercury*, he said. Drunk with his own rhetoric, he declared, 'If Sir you will not leave me alone, I will light such a Torch in England, which it will be out of your power to extinguish: and I will make the year 1809 memorable in the historic Page by the discoveries I shall cause in almost every department in this region. Voltaire has observed to this effect, that Streams always become more impure the farther they are from the fountain Head. I will undertake to prove this assertion just.'

Thomas thought the quotation from Voltaire so apt that he was to use it again later in a letter which did receive the publicity he had in mind, though it did him little good.

This time, however, he had gone too far. On February 6, 1809 he wrote an abject letter of apology to Admiral Sir Alexander Cochrane 'on the anniversary of that memorable day when you gained from Royalty that Title you so eminently adorn'. He reminded him that he had been 'one of the Partners in your Glory, received a Wound which confined me for a length of time to my bed: I received every kind of nourishment and sustenance from your benevolent table and, Oh God, I have made a base return'. This was presumably a reference to the battle of St Domingo when Cochrane distinguished himself as second-in-command to Duckworth and was made a Knight of the Bath for his service. 'Forgiveness Sir is noble...I humbly beg that you will be pleased to accept my contrition and pardon my faults'. His own affairs could not be forgotten for long, 'Patronage is all I want,' said this brazen young man, 'I will undertake to do the rest myself'.

His final sentence removes all doubt as to his mental balance, 'I hope Sir you will not only cause this Letter to be read upon the Quarter Deck of every ship under your command, but publish it in the public Papers, in order that all the World may see my contrition for So enormous an Offence.'

His apology was too late. Thomas's last two commanders had reported that this troublesome purser had kept no accounts whatever; his own comments on this will appear. The admiral could stand only so much, and this gave him the excuse he needed. Reckoning that a court martial would serve no purpose he decided that the best way to rid himself of this pest would be to send him to England. Cochrane ordered that he be superseded and be sent to England in HMS *Acasta*. What the admiral said to Thomas is not recorded, but the man resigned his warrant as acting purser of the *Demerary*.

So three weeks after Thomas had written his threatening letter to Cochrane, he was no longer an officer. He was still in the navy, however, and was ordered to another ship, the *Pelorus*, before the mast, to await passage home.[4] There, thought the admiral, the Victualling Board 'may lay hold of him'.

His disrating prompted another letter to Cochrane, on February 9, 'I do protest, most solemnly protest, against such a proceeding until the Lords of the Admiralty shall have submitted my Case to the King'. Presently he was moved to the *Neptune* as supernumerary.

Brooding over his troubles, unable to go ashore, and living in the rough conditions of all lower deck seamen, Thomas determined that the time had come to light the political fuse which he had long believed he had at his disposal. He decided to write to the Hon. Charles Bragge (afterwards Bragge-Bathurst), one of the MPs for Bristol, the town where he had lived and of which he was a freeman and therefore a voter.

It was now March 24, 1809, and the ex-purser was still having to kick his heels on board HMS *Neptune*, anchored in Fort Royal Bay, Martinique. His letter was a typical mixture of half-truth and invective.[5] He had, he said, resigned his warrant as purser on condition of being discharged from the navy. Yet two ships had left for home while he was still detained, 'kept prisoner' because he had announced his intention to disclose certain matters.

One of these was a scandal on board HMS *Star*. Captain John Simpson, when commanding that ship, had (Thomas alleged) connived at the desertion of a master by making a false muster. Lieutenant Stuart of the *Star* had applied to the admiral to court-martial Captain Simpson, but the only effect of his request was that Cochrane removed Stuart from the ship.

Charles Morgan Thomas, chafing at his continued detention by the admiral, now remembered a story he must surely have heard from James Hobson, from whom he took over in the *Demerary*. It was just what he needed, and he decided to add the Jeffery incident to an exposure of what he considered the scandalous state of affairs in Cochrane's command.

Thomas set down his own situation, and the alleged fraud by the captain of *Star*. He continued, 'I deem it a duty I owe to humanity, to inform you that Capt. Lake, when Commander, of the *Recruit*, set a man belonging to that vessel on shore at Sombrero, an uninhabited island in the Atlantic Archipelago, where he died through hunger, or otherwise, for more was never heard of him. This was likewise known to Sir A. Cochrane, who suffered this *titled murderer* to escape, and he now has the command of the *Ulysses*.'

Here Thomas slipped in his cherished quotation from Voltaire about streams becoming more impure away from the fountain-head. For good measure he then added two more accusations: a transport named *Trinidad* had been employed upon 'speculating purposes' and the ransoming of enemy prisoners had not only been connived at, but encouraged, 'and the honour of the nation has not only been compromised, but basely abandoned, by a set of wretches, calling themselves Commissioned Officers, but who, in reality, would do better behind compters in Cheapside and Ludgate Hill; but if they make these their prototypes, they fall short, very short of the original.'

It was strong stuff. What would have happened if this letter - with no envelope, and sealed only with a wafer - had fallen into the admiral's hands is an interesting question. We do not know what sympathetic messenger took it to England, but someone did, and it arrived safely in the hands of Mr Bragge-Bathurst, MP.

That gentleman passed the letter, or a copy of it, to the Admiralty. Had their Lordships known that Thomas was on the borders of madness, they might well have treated as a wild fiction his extraordinary claim that a naval captain had deliberately abandoned a seaman on a desolate tropical island, and this story would have had a different ending.

Meanwhile Thomas improved the hour by firing off a series of letters to another MP, Samuel Whitbread, the brewer, whom a recent biographer has described as a self-appointed forerunner of the Parliamentary Ombudsman.[6] At this point in what proved to be a long-lasting correspondence, Thomas did not mention the Sombrero incident, but concentrated on his other accusations, such as corruption among pursers, and dishonest ransoming of prizes. The contact with Whitbread, however, was to be an important factor in the way in which the case of Robert Jeffery developed.

The Admiralty had not yet got the measure of their strange informant, Mr Thomas, and on June 6 - that is, virtually at once - the Secretary of the Admiralty, Mr Wellesley Pole, wrote to Captain Lake directing him to explain the Sombrero charge. It probably took some time for this instruction to reach its destination, and the captain's reply was dated from HMS *Ulysses* at the Nore, on July 3, 1809.[7] This was a crucial moment in the war, a few weeks before Arthur Wellesley (brother of Wellesley Pole) was made Viscount Wellington, when warships and transports were being assembled for the ill-fated Scheldt expedition. At the same time the Admiralty had taken the precaution of writing to Admiral Cochrane to ask about Thomas. It took a good deal longer to receive his reply, dated August 4, which must have taken several weeks to reach Whitehall.

By the time it arrived, the past history of their informant

had become irrelevant, for Lake had no choice but to write admitting the charge. By way of justification he simply resorted to blackening the characters of both Jeffery and Thomas. With hyperbole verging on stupidity, he called Robert Jeffery (only just 18 at the time of the Sombrero incident) 'a most infamous character'. As for Charles Morgan Thomas, 'I never saw him; but on enquiry into his character, I am told by the Captains with whom he has sailed, that on account of his improper conduct, he has been obliged to quit two ships, and that he is now serving before the mast in *His Majesty's Ship Neptune'*.

Captain Simpson, formerly of the *Star*, had also been directed to answer the accusation against him; this, and the other charges made by Thomas, need not concern us here. To determine how far Cochrane put other qualities above what we should call integrity in his officers would require a detailed study. The system which required a purser virtually to run his own business on board encouraged dishonesty. An anonymous letter sent to Cochrane about this date warned him that an ex-purser (not Thomas) whom he had caught in peculation had threatened a horse-whipping if he encountered the ex-purser in London. But pursers were more easily dispensed with than fighting officers. The Sombrero incident now took precedence over the rest of Thomas's fulminations for it was a potential political time-bomb. The Admiralty solicitor, Mr Bicknell, was consulted, and gave his opinion that Captain Lake's conduct had been illegal 'however infamous that of the man might have been', and that Lake was liable to a criminal prosecution, a civil action for damages by the victim or to a court martial. (The Crown could not be sued, as the Constitution then stood.)

The Admiralty (and Lake) must have been uncomfortably aware that the case of Robert Jeffery was not without precedent, and a recent precedent at that. Eighteen months earlier, in March 1808, there had been a civil action (Daly v. Rolles) at Kingston assizes in which a midshipman sued his captain for landing him on the desolate island of Lyn Tyn on the coast of China for having 'conducted himself improperly towards his superior officers'. This young man had been better treated than Jeffery, for he was provided with a fowling-piece, powder and provisions, and afterwards came home in an Indiaman. Even so, he was awarded £450 damages.[8]

The Admiralty wrote again to Cochrane before his reply to the first letter had been received, calling for his comments on Thomas's allegation, Captain Lake's admission and the solicitor's opinion.

Meanwhile Thomas himself was on his way back to England in the *Acasta*, and for a brief moment Cochrane must have thought he had heard the last of him. The luckless Thomas - in many ways a pitiable man, and his own enemy - arrived back with only the clothes he stood up in. The rest of his belongings, and the sea-chest in which they were contained, were stolen from him in the *Acasta*.

The ship arrived in the Downs on August 16. On September 5, Thomas was sent to Plymouth Hospital, for he was clearly far from well. The diagnosis was, as ironically it had been with Lake, the catch-all one of 'debility'.[9] Two days later he had once more developed what Cochrane called his 'itch for writing'.[10] This time the Admiralty was the target, but the method was the same: vague threats of disclosures unless he were rehabilitated.

He said he had declined to keep accounts to which he knew himself incompetent to swear 'as invariably is the Case with all Pursers in the West Indies, who have not private fortunes to depend upon...'[11] He was ready to 'divulge the whole proceedings' if he were given an indemnity together with pay and other money which, he claimed, would be due to him on passing his accounts (if, of course, he had kept any).

Their Lordships did not bother to reply, so three weeks later Thomas wrote again. 'I mean not to come forward with old hacknied stories, my information will embrace interests of great magnitude, and I am convinced needs only to be known to be remedied.'[12]

At this point, and quite independently of Thomas's allegations, Lake was in more immediate trouble. Like the *Recruit* earlier, HMS *Ulysses* under Captain Lake was not a happy ship. The indications are that he could not maintain discipline and was apt to drink to excess. As a result he and his officers were at loggerheads. Hobson, who had been acting purser of the *Recruit,* was now Clerk in the *Ulysses.* He was too big for his boots: so much so that one wonders whether he was blackmailing the captain, to whom, presumably, he owed his appointment.

On September 21 Lake had his own first lieutenant, Robert Benjamin Young, court-martialled for drunkenness and contempt.[13] The whole thing was extremely petty. Some misunderstanding over watches had occurred, and Young, a Trafalgar veteran, approached Lake to complain that he was apparently expected to keep the morning watch, 0400-0800, after a full day's work as first lieutenant. The alleged contempt consisted in the manner in which Young, understandably annoyed, had raised his hat to the captain. More relevant to our story is something he said in his defence, 'The very apparent irritation and vexation Captain Lake usually displays in Service, particularly in the evening, and in this instance could so far excite him as to confine me...'

Lieutenant Young was acquitted, and preferred counter-charges against Lake, alleging that he had neglected the discipline of the ship by allowing the officers to be treated with disrespect, of having abused him (Young) and endeavoured to lower him in the opinion of the officers and men, and of repeated drunkenness.

On September 28 and 29, in HMS *Royal Oak* at the Downs, Lake was court-martialled on these charges.[14] Much of the evidence centred round an incident on the evening of July 21, when the *Ulysses* was taking part in the Scheldt expedition, and there was bad feeling over late hours kept in the 'cockpit' by the midshipmen and other inferior officers, including James Hobson the clerk. This affair also seems rather petty, and the fact that there was a court martial at all suggests that the officers at least were driven beyond the limit by the tensions of shipboard life aggravated by the captain's behaviour.

Lake was acquitted on the charge of having neglected discipline and allowing the officers to be treated with disrespect - but the court 'remarked a want of correctness on the part of Lake in not adhering to the...rules of the service.' The charge of having tried to denigrate Lieutenant Young was found part proved and Lake was admonished. On drunkenness he was, perhaps surprisingly, acquitted but 'there appeared to the court to have been irregularity in his conduct on the evening of the July 21 last in having drunk more as it appeared than he usually used to do'.

Lake, defeated, withdrew an application to have another of his officers, the master, court-martialled.

Lieutenant Young was understandably moved from Lake's ship. However, another of the *Ulysses'* lieutenants, George Somerville, had been so exasperated by the insolent behaviour of Hobson, the clerk, that he applied to have him court-martialled also, accusing him of mutinous conduct, disobedience to orders and disrespect. That trial did not take place until January 23, 1810[15], by which time events in connection with the Sombrero affair had moved on. Hobson's trial was held on board *Gladiator* at Portsmouth where the evidence covered much the same ground as the earlier one. Hobson said he did not call the purser a 'bloody bugger', but a 'bloody rogue of a purser...' Lake declared that Hobson's character was 'uncommonly good', and as he told the court that he had reprimanded the clerk, the man got away with an admonishment.

Thomas, still in hospital, wrote three more letters to the Admiralty.[16] On November 10, having had no answer, he told them how his possessions had been stolen, and asked for 'some small pecuniary assistance'. Their Lordships saw no ground for giving him money. Five days later he asked for six weeks' leave or for a new appointment, 'as the Pursers had got scent of him, and it had been hinted to take care of his person' - supposedly because he would expose their swindles. When the Admiralty received this, they ordered the governor of Plymouth Hospital to discharge him if he were fit. The governor said he was not so then, but a fortnight later, on December 8 he was discharged.

He then wrote from an inn at Plymouth to ask for his back pay since he had ceased to be a purser.[17] (Pursers were not paid until they had accounted to the Victualling Board for the stores in their charge. Thomas had admitted no such accounts existed, and made no attempt to claim pay for his time as purser.) He was told he could have his pay as supernumerary, £11, if he claimed it at the Plymouth Pay Office.

Like Cochrane earlier, the Admiralty may have hoped they had heard the last of Thomas. However, that strange person now revealed himself as an inventor. He had put up at the Navy Hotel, in Fore Street, Plymouth, and wrote to the Admiralty on December 15 with a plan for destroying Napoleon's invasion flotilla at Boulogne 'without risk to ourselves of a single Ship and probably not many lives'. This was to be done by firing rockets from boats of a special design which he had invented. These were to consist of a hull, with sharply-pointed stem and stern, decked with stout planks which would project nine or ten feet on either side. A small scuttle would provide the only entrance to the hull, and when loaded with men and stores the hull would sink to water level, kept afloat only by the wide projecting deck. The boats would be fitted with two masts and lugsails, and would be towed across the Channel, then allowed to drift at the end of a long line towards the French shore with the tide. When within range, they would fire their rockets into Boulogne, then be hauled back to the towing warships. The French gunners would be baffled because the raft-like boats would present virtually no target above water-level.

The Admiralty dismissed the idea as 'too absurd to deserve notice'. One wonders whether the later generation which saw such inventions as the Mulberry Harbour and Pluto would have been so cavalier.

Meanwhile Admiral Cochrane had replied to the Admiralty's formal direction to look into the Sombrero affair. Newly promoted to vice-admiral, he wrote to Wellesley Pole from HMS *Pompée* at Halifax, Nova Scotia, on November 1.[18] This was the letter in which he made it clear that he was 'well aware of the irregularity of the proceeding' (the landing of Jeffery on the island) and how, after being 'assured' of his safety by an American newspaper report, he consented after 'seriously admonishing' Lake to let the business rest. If their Lordships should decide to try Lake by court martial there were many persons still in the *Recruit* who no doubt could prove the circumstances. 'Though,' the admiral added, 'the situation of the island of Sombrero is close to Anguilla, and in the track where vessels are constantly passing and re-passing.'

Their Lordships decided that, with the *Recruit* now in home waters, three captains, the usual formula for a naval inquiry, should board her and interview personnel who had been serving at the time of the incident. This they did at Portsmouth on December 9, 1809.[19] The three captains - Richard Lee, William Bedford and John E. Douglas - examined the muster book (which still showed Jeffery as Run) and also the log (presumably the master's log), which contained an entry showing that Jeffery had been landed on the island. They took statements from several petty officers still serving in the ship: Joseph Elvey, clerk, Thomas Jenkins, serjeant of Marines, Joseph Mott, captain of the forecastle, John Pearson, quartermaster, and Francisco Valla, one of the boat's crew at the time. All confirmed both the landing and the fruitless search made two months later.

The officers who had served with Lake were now dispersed, but the purser, a man named H. G. Windsor, who joined just after Lake left (in June 1808) made a statement based on his conversations with the then master, Edward Spencer, and other former members of the gun-room mess who had been present at the time.[20] The landing had been considered by all the officers to have been very cruel and when publicly spoken of, an act of oppression.

With these statements, the Admiralty saw that a court martial of Captain Lake was unavoidable. *Ulysses*, like *Recruit,* was in British waters. Sufficient witnesses were to hand - though not, predictably, Charles Morgan Thomas. On January 4, 1810, search was made for him at Plymouth to warn him he would be required to give evidence but he could not be found, and there was no trace of him (not even another letter) until a month after the court martial was over.[21]

The Judge Advocate of the Fleet was the Right Honourable Nathaniel Bond, but whose office more often than not was carried out by his appointed deputy. For courts martial held at Portsmouth and Plymouth, it was usual for a prominent local attorney to fill this role, a combination of legal advisor to the court and prosecuting lawyer. It is perhaps symptomatic of the navy's wish to play down the Sombrero case that the Judge Advocate of the Fleet did not prosecute in person as he would have done had the accused been a flag officer. The trial of Captain Lake was to be held at Portsmouth, and Nathaniel Bond left the task to his usual deputy there, a notary and attorney named Moses Greetham, junior.[22]

The admiral commanding Spithead and Portsmouth station, Sir Roger Curtis, had been directed not to open the court until the arrival of Charles Morgan Thomas and Edward Spencer.[23] The Deputy Judge Advocate, Moses Greetham, told the Admiralty that Thomas could not give any first hand evidence so there was no point in waiting for him to turn up. Spencer by now (January 15) had already arrived. He had said that the order to land Jeffery had been given to Lieutenant Mould on the quarter deck, but not in the hearing of anyone else. Greetham now thought that the giving of the order might have to be proved. If Mould were in England 'and his Attendance can be conveniently procured' it might be desirable to call him.

The tentative and subservient way in which all this was put shows the weakness of the legal advice offered to the Admiralty on the case. Admiral Curtis at least was more alert to the need for the prosecution not to fail. He told Greetham to point out that another witness, Joseph Elvey, former clerk of HMS *Recruit*, who had testified at the inquiry, had since been discharged from the navy by Admiralty order on December 20, having been claimed as an apprentice.

Mould was in fact serving in HMS *St Alban's*, in which he had sailed to the Far East, and to recall him would require several months delay. The new Secretary of the Admiralty, Croker, minuted upon the Deputy Judge Advocate's letter that Lieutenant Mould was understood not to be in England, but inquiries were being made for him, as well as for Elvey. However, 'it was apprehended' that as Lake had admitted giving the order Mould's evidence would be of minimal importance. Mould, of course, had obeyed Captain Lake and landed Jeffery. The question of whether he could validly plead 'superior orders' was not even raised. It would have been unjust to postpone the trial longer than absolutely necessary so it was decided to go ahead without him. Nevertheless, he had been one of the key actors in the whole affair, and curiously it was Lake who afterwards wished to have been able to question him. Mould did not return to England until July 1810.

At the last minute, on January 20, Lake succeeded in getting a short postponement of the trial so that he could bring as witness a man named George Wilson, second mate of a merchant ship called the *Ann* of Glasgow.[24] Wilson was understood to have seen Jeffery since the landing. In the event it seems that he could not be found - at any rate he did not appear - and orders were given for the trial to proceed.

Chapter 5

DISMISSED THE SERVICE

On February 5, 1810 the Sombrero court martial assembled in the big cabin of HMS *Gladiator* in Portsmouth harbour. According to custom, the president was the one of the senior officers in the Spithead and Portsmouth command, Captain William Bedford, of the *Caledonia*. If normal practice was followed, he sat at the head of the large table, with the 12 other post-captains who comprised the court on either side of him by seniority. At the bottom of the table, nearest the entrance, was the place of the Judge Advocate.

The prisoner, Captain Lake, was brought in. He and the 'friend' he was allowed to bring with him would have sat near Greetham, the deputy judge advocate. His sword would be placed upon the table, transversely in front of him. The prisoner's friend, in fact, could be a lawyer. The minutes show that later in the hearing Captain Lake was allowed to have his defence statement read by 'his friend Mr Best, a barrister'. This is the only indication that he had legal assistance at the trial, but his counsel appears not to have played any direct part in the proceedings. It is fair to assume, however, that Lake received advice on his line of defence and on questions he might put to witnesses.

There was only one member of the Bar named Best at this period, and this was a fairly distinguished one - William Draper Best, a serjeant-at-law and MP for Petersfield who later became a judge and (as Chief Justice of the Common Pleas) was created a peer as Lord Wynford. Not a learned lawyer, he was an intelligent and fluent advocate, if somewhat hasty.

In the words of the official minute, the 'audience' was then admitted; it is not known whether any member of the public was bold enough to attend. The Admiralty order which convened the court martial was next read. It outlined the original letter from Charles Thomas, and the report of the December enquiry.

The 13 members of the court and the judge advocate took both the judicial oath and an oath to keep secret the deliberations and individual votes of the court.[1] The relevant documents were then read, beginning with Thomas's letter to Bragge-Bathurst and ending with Admiral Cochrane's letter to the Admiralty.

At this point Captain Lake handed in a statement submitting that he had never denied landing Jeffery and, to save the time of the court, that he was now willing to admit it. The court was cleared to allow its members to consider this forthright admission. The captains decided that it was necessary for the court to hear evidence of the facts to enable them to form their own judgement of the case. (The court martial was 'to enquire into the conduct' of Lake on the occasion of the incident and 'to try him for having ordered and caused the said Robert Jeffery to be landed' on the island at the date and time stated. The circumstances had to be established.)

Seven witnesses were called by the prosecution. All had been serving in HMS *Recruit* in December 1807: the master, Edward Spencer; two who were rated as boys, Joseph Elvey and Francisco Valla; the acting purser, James Hobson; Thomas Jenkins, serjeant of marines; John Pearson, quartermaster; and the captain of the forecastle, Joseph Mott. All agreed on the main facts: how Lake had called Jeffery on deck, had ordered him to be landed, how the landing took place, and how the subsequent search revealed no trace of the man. The procedure was slow and tedious, each question and answer being written down in longhand.

The first and principal witness was the master, Spencer. His evidence was detailed and lengthy. In reply to the judge advocate he recounted the basic story, and was then questioned by members of the court, and later by the defendant, Lake. From his replies two or three tentative conclusions may be reached.

1 Much of what Spencer had to say reflected badly upon himself both as a possible conspirator with Lake to 'get rid of' Jeffery and also as a supposedly competent navigating officer. It seems at least possible that he had been granted immunity in return for his evidence.

2 Spencer sought to mitigate Lake's conduct where he could, and by not volunteering statements which would blacken him, while accepting no blame himself.

3 Some members of the court did their best to elicit evidence that Lake thought the island was inhabited and that none of his officers had regarded his act so cruel that they should intercede on Jeffery's behalf. While being questioned by the court Spencer produced his curious story that he had inserted a sentence in his log recording the landing of Jeffery, because this had been omitted by the master's mate who wrote up the book for him. About several points Spencer expressed a degree of vagueness which, if genuine, was remarkable in a naval master whose position required him to be a trained observer and who, having passed an examination by Trinity House, was directly responsible to the commander for the ship's navigation. We have already seen that at the time of the incident he had no navigational manual for the West Indies.

Q: What is the nearest inhabited island to Sombrero?

Spencer: To the best of my knowledge, I think it is Anguilla, which is, I believe seven or eight leagues distant

(The distance is in fact 38 miles - more than 12 leagues. In a later question Spencer was asked what distance was the island of Anegada from Sombrero. His reply was 'I suppose nearly 10 or 11 leagues'. It is actually 55 miles - more than 18 leagues.)

Q: At what distance do vessels generally pass from the island of Sombrero?

A: I have heard they pass near, but never saw them; the *Recruit* was within a quarter of a mile from Sombrero; the channel is about five or six leagues across, and I have heard that the French fishermen come there turtling.

Q: Had any steps been taken to ascertain if there were any inhabitants on the island previous to Jeffery being ordered to be landed there, or provisions or water?

A: I do not know.

Q: Do you know that there were any eggs or young birds in the island in the month of December, or was it likely, from your observations, that there were any at the time?

A: I do not know that there were any, but I think it is very likely.

Q: Did Lieutenant Mould, or any other officer, point out to Captain Lake what would be the probable fate of Jeffery on that day or the following?

A: Not that I heard.

And again,

Q: From your knowledge of the trade-wind in the West Indies, and the Dog and Prickly Pear Passage (which separates Sombrero from Anguilla), did it strike your mind as probable that vessels would pass near enough to discover Jeffery on the island of Sombrero?

A: Yes, it did, at the time.

Q: Did you, or any of the officers, to your knowledge, request Captain Lake to send for Jeffery, on the morning of the 14th, the island then in sight?

A: I did not; neither did I hear any of the other officers.

And a little later,

Q: Did you at any subsequent period afterwards (following the search made in February) hear Captain Lake express any apprehensions as to the fate of Jeffery?

A: Not to the best of my recollection, except as I have before stated.

Q: Have you any reason to think, from Captain Lake's saying that he supposed Jeffery had got housed, that he believed the island of Sombrero to be inhabited?

A: I really believe he did.

Q: Was you prevented by fear, or any other motive, from suggesting to Captain Lake the taking off [of] Jeffery?

A: No, I was not.

Q: Did Lieutenant Mould give his opinion as to the propriety of leaving Jeffery on the island?

A: Not that I heard.

Captain Lake now cross-examined. First he took up the implication by Spencer that because he (the master) had not named the 'two thieves', it was Lake who identified Jeffery as one of them. Lake now asked Spencer straight out:

Q: You said, 'We have two thieves on board.' Did you mean Jeffery was one?

A: I did.

Lake also scotched two more of Spencer's attempts to distance himself:

Q: Did you often report Jeffery to me as a very bad character, and say it would be a very good thing if we could get him out of the ship; that flogging would do him no good?

A: Yes; I did.

Q: Did you conceive, at the time he was landed, that there were houses, or rocks appearing like houses, on the island?

A: At the time I thought there were houses, and did not know that it was not inhabited.

A member of the court restored the balance on the latter point:

Q: Considering the description you have given of the island, and the situation of your ship, could you, or any other officer of the ship, have discovered houses, if there had been any there?

A: No, we could not. I think there might have been houses and we not see them; the land rises from the surface of the water above 40 feet, I should think, and therefore we could not see over the island.

One of the captains probed further into Spencer's opinion of Jeffery,

Q: Why had you frequently complained of Jeffery to Captain Lake, and wish him out of the ship?

A: He was generally down below in the watch and could never be got up on deck. He had not been long at sea; he was a very weak man; and his punishments hurt him very much; and I thought such a man had better be out of the ship. I do not mean his flogging; he was started several times by a boatswain's mate with a rope.

Before Spencer left the witness-stand that day he made

further replies which strongly suggest that, morally at least, he should have been on trial himself.

Q: What in your conscience was the impression upon your mind, at the time that Jeffery was landed on Sombrero, whether it was a desolate island or not?

A: The impression on my mind was, I did not think it a desolate island.

Q: Had you any reason to alter that opinion on the return of the boat with Lieutenant Mould, or before you lost sight of the island?

A: No.

Q: Did you then consider the act of Captain Lake as very oppressive?

A: I did not consider whether it was oppressive or not. I did not take it into consideration.

Spencer said he had been a master since March, 1807, and served years in the West Indies in a man-of-war 'and never was in sight of the island before we landed the man, to the best of my knowledge'.

Q: Did you ever look to see if Sombrero was inhabited, or had wood or water?

A: No; I never did.

Q: Was the *Recruit* in want of water at the time?

A: I do not recollect.

The next witness was Joseph Elvey, a boy seaman from London, who had been a member of the *Recruit*'s afterguard. His evidence was unhelpful. Although he had seen Jeffery go into the boat, he was hesitant on detail of the lad's clothing.

His replies to almost all other questions put to him were that he did not know, had not heard or did not recollect. He even evaded the character question: 'Was Jeffery considered an infamous character?' by simply saying that he had been flogged once for taking rum out of the gunner's cabin. He did, however, agree to the leading question put by a member of the court,

Q: Did you think it a very very cruel and oppressive act, at the time the putting Jeffery on shore?

A: Yes, I did.

Francesco Valla, a Maltese lad, despite being an officer's servant had been in the crew of the boat which landed Robert Jeffery. He was a much better witness, although he too was only about 16 at the time. He gave a clear and graphic description of the events of that evening. Members of the boat's crew had gone ashore at Sombrero with Lieutenant Mould and, Valla stated in reply to one of the captains, when they came down they said there were no houses.

Next came James Hobson, who had been acting purser of the *Recruit*, and as we have seen may have been a favourite - or blackmailer - of Captain Lake, with whom he was now serving again in HMS *Ulysses*. Hobson was asked some fairly pointed questions by the judge advocate about the entries concerning Jeffery in the muster book, which was his responsibility.

Judge Advocate: By whose order did you put the 'R' against his name?

Hobson: I believe I did it of my own accord.

Q: Did Captain Lake know that you had so done?

A: When the ship arrived at Barbados he asked me how he was discharged on the book: I told him I had run him on the books; he said that I ought to have discharged him to Sombrero.

Admiral Sir Alexander Cochrane 1824
National Portrait Gallery, London
Sir Francis Burdett, by Adam Buck c1810

An Account of the Dreadful Hardships and Sufferings of

ROBERT JEFFERY, a British Seaman,

Who was cruelly put on Shore on a desolate Island, which affords no article of human Food, where, after many days residence, he was at last providentially picked up, in the last stage of Starvation, by an American vessel.

THE story of Jeffery, the seaman, having excited considerable interest, on account of the perilous situation in which he was left on a desert island by Capt. Lake, of his Majesty's brig Recruit, and the uncertainty respecting his fate; we are now happy in being able to give a good and satisfactory account of him.

Robert Jeffery was born at Polperro, in the county of Cornwall, in Great Britain, where he was educated, and instructed in reading, writing, and common arithmetic. Here also he learnt the business of a blacksmith, and kept a daily journal of work done in the shop.

Having a desire to go to sea, in the summer of 1807, he shipped himself, at Polperro on board the privateer schooner, Lord Nelson, of Plymouth. About eight days afterwards the schooner put into Falmouth, where he was impressed by an officer, belonging to his Britannic Majesty's brig Recruit, of 18 guns, commanded by Capt. Lake, and carried on board that ship; where he was appointed Armourer's mate, and soon afterwards sailed in the Recruit for the West Indies, where she cruised about three months. The brig's water running short, the crew were allowanced, and Jeffery being very thirsty, and unable to obtain a sufficiency to quench his thirst, one Saturday evening went to the beer cask, and drew off about two quarts into a bucket, drank about three-quarters of it, and left the remainder in the bucket; one of the crew was present when this took place, and informed Capt. Lake of it, who next day asked Jeffery if it was he who tapped the beer, to which he replied in the affirmative, and Capt. Lake ordered the Serjeant of Marines to put him on the black list.

Jeffery continued to his duty as usual, and nothing else particular ocurred until the Sunday following, Captain Lake called him aft, and said to him (Sombrero island being then in sight)—'Jeffery, do you see that island; do you know that I am going to land you on it?' To which he replied in the negative.— Shortly afterwards Captain Lake ordered the boat to be lowered down; the second Lieutenant, a Midshipman, and four men, to land him on Sombrero island.

Jeffery wished to take his clothes with him, but Captain Lake denied him them, or any thing else, except what he then had upon him, and when the boat landed him, the rocks cut his feet; upon which the Lieutenant begged one of the men in the boat to spare him a pair of shoes, which he did, and gave him a knife; the Lieutenant and Midshipman each gave him a handkerchief, and left him on the island of Sombrero aforesaid; the

Lieutenant having previously recommended him to keep a look out for vessels passing.

Sombrero is a desolate island, without any inhabitant thereon, or sustenance of any kind to support life, and he remained on it nine days without any food, save about a dozen of limpits, that he picked off the rocks: his drink was sometimes salt water, at other times rain water, which he found in crevices of the rocks after a fall of rain.

He saw several vessels pass, and attempted to hail them, but without effect, for they were too distant to hear or see him, until the schooner Adams, of Marblehead, John Dennis, Master, came to his assistance, took him off, and landed him at Marblehead, in the county of Essex, and State of Massachusetts, in the United States of America.

An account of this cruel affair having reached this country through the medium of an American paper, an investigation of the affair was immediately instituted. Capt. Lake was tried for the offence before a Court Martial; when he was reprimanded and dismissed his Majesty's service. Still the fate of Jeffery remained to be ascertaind, and various reports were circulated respecting him. At length appeared a declaration and affidavit made by Jeffery himself, before a justice of the peace at Wenham, in Essex, in the state of Massachusetts, in presence of his Britannic Majesty's Consul, dated 27th. June, 1810; which seemed to satisfy the Public mind respecting his safety. Some doubts however were yet entertained on account of this affidavit being signed with a cross, as Jeffery was known to be well able to write his own name. All these doubts and fears were happily removed by his arrival at London on Monday last. (Oct. 22, 1810.)

Jeffery confirms the truth of the above account, and adds, that he was in the very last stage of starvation when the American vessel touched at the island. The Lords of the Admiralty have given him a free discharge from the service; and the friends of Capt. Lake made him what they deemed a compensation for the hardships he has sustained. He is a good-looking young man, about 22 years of age; and says that though he can write, he signed the affidavit with a cross, for shortness, as is customary amongst sailors.

He left London on Tuesday, in high spirits, with his money, to see his mother, who lives at Polperro, in Cornwall. Some people were after him, to make him exhibit himself for money; but this he could not comply with, as he got his discharge from the service expressly on the condition that he should immediately quit London.

Broadsheet account of Jeffery's story, October 1810
Neville Jolliff

AN ACCOUNT OF THE SUFFERINGS OF

Jeffery the Seaman,

DURING HIS ABODE ON THE DESOLATE ROCK, OF

SOMBRERO

WHERE HE WAS LEFT
BY THE INHUMAN ORDER OF HIS CAPTAIN.
EXTRACTED FROM

A JOURNAL OR DAIRY,

DURING THE EIGHT DAYS HE REMAINED THERE.

*With JEFFERY's Affidavit of his usage by he Captain,
And the particulars of the affectionate Meeting of Jeffery and
his Mother on his return to England.*

Who is now to be seen at Mr. Wigley's Exibition room, Spring gardens.

Printed and Sold by *J. Pitts, No. 14, Great St. Andrew-street*
Seven Dials.

[PRICE ONE PENNY.]

Handbill advertising Jeffery's exhibition, 1811
(Courtesy of the Essex Institute, Salem, Mass.)

A

REPRESENTATION

LARGE AS LIFE,

OF

J E F F E R Y

LANDING ON THE ISLAND OF

SOMBRERO,

BY ORDER OF

CAPTAIN LAKE.

THE RECRUIT BRIG, IS AT A DISTANCE;

THE SMALL BOAT,

HAVING PUT JEFFERY ON THE ROCK,

IS RETURNING;

Whilst the Victim, with fixed eyes and clasped hands,
is seen in an agony of Distress ! ! !

ADMITTANCE ONE SHILLING.

N. B. THE PICTURE IS SHEWN BY

JEFFERY HIMSELF,

AT WIGLEY'S ROOMS, SPRING GARDENS,

CHARING CROSS.

May 27, 1811.

Handbill advertising Jeffery's exhibition, 1811
(Courtesy of the Essex Institute, Salem, Mass.)

Q: How long was that afterwards?

A: About six weeks ago (*sic*). (Can the witness have meant 'six weeks afterwards', ie after the landing?)

Q: Did Captain Lake direct you to take out the 'R' and make an entry of his being discharged to Sombrero?

A: Yes.

Q: Why did you not do it?

A: Because I believe I had sent a muster book up previous.

Q: Had Captain Lake any knowledge of that muster book having been sent away, and of the 'R' having remained against the name of Jeffery on that book?

A: He signed that book, but he did not know that the 'R' was against Jeffery's name at the time it was sent.

Q: Before you had entered the 'R' against the name of Jeffery, had you any conversation with Captain Lake, as to the mode the entry should be made on the book?

A: No.

Members of the court asked Hobson what had become standard questions. He said he thought Sombrero was inhabited because he heard the two lieutenants and, he thought, the master say that fishermen resorted to it; and he understood that it was always inhabited by some of them.

He heard Lieutenant Mould say, after landing Jeffery, that he (Mould) did not think the island was inhabited. 'I have no knowledge that it was stated to Captain Lake.'

Q: Did you, at any period subsequent to December 13, 1807, hear Captain Lake express apprehension respecting the fate of Jeffery?

A: No; only when he learnt it was an uninhabited island, he said he was very sorry it had happened; he would rather have given £20,000. This was after he had been to the admiral, at Barbados.

Q: Do you know when Captain Lake heard that Sombrero was not inhabited?

A: I believe he heard it when we got to Barbados.

Q: Did Captain Lake tell you so?

A: Captain Lake told me he understood that it was an uninhabited island and that he was going back to see if the man was there, by the admiral's orders.

Q: How long have you sailed with Captain Lake?

A: From March 6, 1806 to June 14, 1808, and from May 30, 1809 to this date.

Q: From your knowledge of Captain Lake, do you think he would have ordered Jeffery to have been put on Sombrero if he knew it was uninhabited?

A: No; I am almost sure he would not.

Q: Do you know if Captain Lake, at the time Jeffery was put on shore, directed any enquiry to be made whether the island was inhabited or not?

A: If he did I never heard of it.

Captain Lake, cross-examining, attempted unsuccessfully to implicate the absent second lieutenant by asking,

Q: Did you hear Lieutenant Mould ask me leave to go and land the man, volunteering to do it?

A: No, I was below.

Next day, February 6, Spencer was recalled for more questions by the court. Asked whether Lake, at the time Jeffery was landed, had given directions to find out whether the island was inhabited, he echoed Hobson's answer, 'Not that I heard'.

The court then devoted some effort to finding out why Lake had sent for his pistols, and what his state of mind might have been.

Q: At the time Captain Lake ordered his pistols to be brought on deck did you notice the state of his mental faculties?

A: No. I did not.

Q: Had you any reason, from his conduct, to suspect him not to be of sound mind at the time?

A: I did not consider myself a competent judge, but I have heard the surgeon say, that he thought he was a little touched, or insane. At the time he ordered the pistols to be brought on deck, he spoke loud and harsh. I think he was as much in his senses then as he usually was, when carrying on the duty of the ship.

Spencer said he had seen the pistols brought up so often that he could not remember whether this had occurred only when beating the quarters. He did not know whether on this occasion they were loaded.

Q: Relate to the court whether Captain Lake was sober on the evening of December 13, 1807 when he ordered Jeffery to be put on shore on Sombrero:

A: I do not think he was perfectly sober.

Q: In one part of your evidence you say that the conduct of Captain Lake was as usual at the time Jeffery was sent on shore, and you have since said that you do not think he was perfectly sober - what are the Court to understand from that?

A: Captain Lake, after his wine, was usually more elevated than he was in the former part of the day.

The next witness was Thomas Jenkins, Serjeant of Marines, a 30-year-old Mancunian. He had brought up Jeffery when the captain had called for him. He was asked rather naively why he did not bring up the lad's clothes, and gave the answer which might have been expected, 'I was never ordered to bring them up'.

Serjeant Jenkins seems to have been honest if unimaginative. He himself thought the island was inhabited because the rocks upon it appeared like houses. A member of the court asked him whether Jeffery was considered as an infamous character on board. No, said the serjeant, he was confined about a week before for theft. When people were saying that Jeffery would be starved to death on the island, he heard Spencer say 'You be damned' -'which I thought meant he would do very well'. He was asked a remarkably leading question about Lake's state of mind,

Q: Did you notice anything extraordinary in the conduct of Captain Lake, at the time he sent Jeffery on shore; or did he carry on the duty in a cool, deliberate manner, in his usual way?

A: He appeared to be very passionate at the time, more than usual.

Q: From what you observed at the time, have you any reason to believe that he was not of sound mind at the time when he sent Jeffery on shore?

A: No, I do not know. He was not in such a passion in the morning as he was overnight.

But, on the evening when Jeffery was landed, the captain had appeared to be sober.

John Pearson, a 22-year-old Geordie seaman, had been

quartermaster's mate in December, 1807. When Jeffery was brought up, Pearson he met him coming along the main-deck, and remembered clearly what the lad was wearing. The court asked,

Q: Was he considered an infamous character?

A: He had a good character, as far as I know.

Q: What impression did it make on your mind, the landing of Jeffery; did you think it an act of cruelty and oppression?

A: I thought it was a very cruel thing at the time. (Asked what induced him to think so, Pearson replied that the people were saying at the time that it was a barren island; he himself did not know what island it was.)

The last witness was another seaman, Joseph Mott, from Lynn in Norfolk, who less than a fortnight before the incident, had been promoted captain of the forecastle; he was then 25. He could add little. Pearson had said it was light enough that evening to see houses and smoke on Sombrero, had there been any; he saw none. Mott, however, had been in the boat's crew and said there were rocks that looked like houses, but they did not seem so when they got round the island. He was asked the usual question,

Q: What impression had it on your mind at the time, leaving Jeffery behind?

A: I thought it was very sorrowful to see a man left on a desolate island like that.

Q: Did you think it a cruel act?

A: Yes.

Q: Did you know it was a desolate island?

A: No; it was dusk. I did not think it was cruel at first; but when we returned, and found it to be a desolate island, I thought so.

He, too, remembered Lieutenant Mould saying it was a barren place, as he came over the gangway, but did not hear Mould tell Captain Lake so.

Q: Did you see Captain Lake when he ordered Jeffery to be landed?

A: Yes.

Q: Did you then consider him to be in his right senses?

A: The same as usual, only passionate

This concluded the evidence for the prosecution. Lake called no witnesses but had written a long statement which his counsel, Mr Best, now read to the court.

The accusation had been brought, Lake reiterated, by 'a person I have never seen in my life, but whose character will not bear investigation'. He had never denied having landed Jeffery, but 'do from my heart deny the motives imputed to me.'

'I solemnly declare, I never intended to put Robert Jeffery in any jeopardy by landing him. It appears that his character was bad; his propensity to disobedience and dishonesty was such as to lead me and others to believe that punishment would only harden his heart, and confirm him in his bad practices.' Spencer had advised him to get the man out of the ship, and 'I declare, that by landing him, I thought he would be made more sensible of his want of conduct, and reform in future. I was persuaded, at the time, that the island was inhabited; in addition to which, I cannot but suppose it within your knowledge, that the island is not out of the reach of human assistance.'

Lake's next statement was remarkable for its insensitivity.

Vessels, he said, frequently passed within sail (sic) of the island: 'Jeffery found this to be the case, and there is no reason to doubt but that he was taken off the island; for it appears, that on a search being made there afterwards for him, one of the witnesses states expressly that not a trace of him was to be found which I cannot conceive could have been the case if he had perished there, as is most unwarrantably asserted by Thomas.

'Gentlemen, I have no doubt he was conveyed to America in perfect safety. I myself verily believe he is in England at this moment, consigned (as it were) to the merchants, out of whose service I pressed him, and who, perhaps, are keeping him concealed till the event of this court martial is known, and then he may be let loose upon me, to seek a compensation in damages, by an action at law; the place of his concealment, however, has hitherto eluded the diligence of my agents.'

Lake complained that he was considerably disadvantaged because several witnesses, whom he considered material on his behalf, were abroad, such as Lieutenant Mould, Midshipman Salmond, Boyce the gunner and others, including Captain Crofton (who had claimed to have seen the newspaper report that Jeffery had been rescued and taken to America).

He cited in his defence the report made by Admiral Cochrane, 'wherein he expresses himself fully satisfied as to the man's safety'. Cochrane had decided no court martial was necessary but had admonished him. He (Lake) had hoped 'this unfortunate event had been sufficiently visited and that the present court martial might have been deemed unnecessary'.

He recalled recognition which had been given to him on some earlier occasion (unspecified), and claimed that the evidence vindicated him from the charge of being 'cruel and oppressive'.

Finally, he disclosed a testimonial letter, dated only the previous day (when his conviction must have seemed inevitable), and signed by five officers of his present ship, HMS

Ulysses. In the light of previous events, and notably the court martial of five months before, it contains some remarkable statements,

'In our opinion your general conduct has been particularly marked by kindness and humanity, in every respect becoming the character of a British Officer, anxious for the welfare, comfort and happiness (where misrepresentation did not exist) of those placed under your command; and further, that we have reason to conclude anything like preconcerted or deliberate cruelty or oppression totally foreign to your natural disposition.

'We are confident that those to whom we are known will readily acquit our conduct, on this occasion, of anything pertaining to flattery or insincerity.'

The signatories were, Lieutenant George Robinson; John J. Crout, master (whom Lake had been seeking to have court-martialled, though he had later withdrawn his charges); John Thompson, surgeon; John Marsh Luett, purser, and Lieutenant A. Campbell, Royal Marines.

At the end of the statement read by Lake's counsel the court rose. When it reassembled, the position of Lake's sword (surrendered and placed on the table at the beginning of the hearing) would probably have been changed so that its point was towards him, the traditional sign of a guilty verdict. The members of the court, in full dress uniform, would have put on their cocked hats for the reading of the formal sentence, 'having maturely and deliberately weighed and considered the whole, the Court is of opinion, That the Charge has been proved against the said Hon. Warwick Lake, and doth adjudge him to be dismissed from His Majesty's service'.

Orders were given that the name of Warwick Lake be entered in the Admiralty Black Book of officers not to be employed again because of misconduct.[2]

Had Captain Lake, now in the expressive phrase of the time 'broken' by court martial, acted with deliberate cruelty in landing Jeffery or, as seems more likely, in a drunken rage? Had he undergone a belated change, perhaps after his first court martial, into the kindly father of his crew that his latest colleagues described? That does seem hard to believe, and we cannot know what view the members of the court may have taken on the point, if they considered it at all, for it was not the custom of courts martial to give reasoned judgements. In any event this was far from the end of the story. If the former Captain Warwick Lake expected to retire to obscurity, he was to be disappointed.

Chapter 6

POLITICIANS' FIELD-DAY

Circumstances combined to make the spring of 1810 exactly the time when the case of Jeffery the Seaman could be turned to advantage as a stick to beat the Tory Government. It had been, of course, a letter to a Member of Parliament by the egregious Charles Thomas which had first brought the case to light in England. By that time Thomas had already begun to write to Samuel Whitbread on other alleged abuses in the navy. Although Whitbread remained Thomas's preferred contact, the man who now took the political initiative was Sir Francis Burdett, the radical reformer. Burdett was one of the two MPs for Westminster - the other being Thomas Cochrane, nephew of Vice-Admiral Sir Alexander Cochrane (as he now was).

The trial had taken place on Monday and Tuesday, February 5 and 6. Newspaper reports began to appear at once. *The Times* published a brief item on Wednesday, February 7[1] which covered only the first day's proceedings. For the defence, verdict and sentence, *Times* readers were kept waiting until the following Tuesday, February 13.[2]

Burdett read the reports, and on Thursday, February 15 he rose in the House of Commons to make members aware of the case, and asked whether the ministry meant to take any steps in regard to it.[3] If they did not, he would. Apparently he had known nothing of it until then, and accepted that news of the landing of Jeffery had reached the government through American newspaper stories: very much a half-truth.

Robert Plumer Ward, a civil lord of the Admiralty, was in the House and immediately stone-walled. He himself knew nothing of the business except that which related to the court martial. Lake's sentence of dismissal had been carried into effect, and the Board of Admiralty had no power to do more.

Burdett called for an emergency debate on the case, but Speaker Abbot told him firmly that this could only be granted if Sir Francis had some definite notice or motion to put to the House. Burdett began to wax eloquent about matters of life and death, and the lives and liberties of English seamen, but he was shouted down, and said he would take a day or two to think about the best form in which to bring the case before the House.

Hardly surprisingly, the Government did nothing except presumably to acquiesce in a Commons order that the minutes of the court martial be laid before the House.[4] On February 23 Sir Francis rose again to call for a copy of the court martial minutes. These, together with the associated papers, were then made available to Members and ordered to be printed.[5] This in effect meant their release also to the press, and papers from *The Times* to Cobbett's weekly *Political Register* published reports. Cobbett, in fact, published all the documents verbatim in his issues of March 17 and March 24, 1810.[6]

The story of 'Jeffery the Seaman' became known up and down the country. It was both a *cause célèbre* and a popular drama, with no conclusion in sight, for whatever Lake might say the whereabouts and even the survival of Jeffery remained unknown.

The Government still remained supine, hoping (as so many had already done) that the furore would die down.

Sir Francis Burdett was not the man to retreat when he had a weapon against the Government of this calibre. At his demand, on Tuesday, April 3, the case of Captain Lake and Robert Jeffery was given a full debate in the Commons.[7] The House met in St Stephen's Chapel, as Charles Thomas reminded us by his threat to visit it. The chapel, burned with the rest of the Parliament buildings in 1834, was slightly smaller than the present chamber. Its site is exactly covered by the present St Stephen's Hall, through which visitors to the Commons pass.

The attack was led by the three most prominent opposition Members: Sir Francis Burdett, Samuel Whitbread and Lord Folkestone. On the Government side, the Prime Minister, Spencer Perceval, decided to play a leading part himself. The only other cabinet minister present in the House was the Home Secretary, Richard Ryder. The First Lord of the Admiralty, Lord Mulgrave, was a peer, so the Admiralty was represented in the debate by two other Lords Commissioners, Sir Richard Bickerton and Robert Plumer Ward, in addition to John Wilson Croker, the Secretary of the Admiralty (then a political office), and Hon. William Wellesley Pole, whom Croker had succeeded in October 1809. As if that were not enough, there were two veteran admirals, Sir Eliab Harvey and Sir Charles Morice Pole (MP for Plymouth), and a distinguished naval captain, John Poo Beresford.

James Buller, one of the two Members for West Looe, and a capital burgess of that borough, was in a difficult position. Polperro was only three miles from Looe, so that in a sense he was more a local MP than the representatives of the county as a whole. However, he was also a Lord of the Admiralty so wisely took no part in the debate (if he were even present). The other MP for West Looe, Ralph Allen Daniell, likewise took no part, nor did the Members for Cornwall, Sir William Lemon and John Hearle Tremayne, both county gentlemen with no naval background.

Sir Francis Burdett (Westminster) opened the debate with a strong speech proposing a motion that a select committee be appointed 'to consider the papers relating to the conduct and trial of the Hon. Captain Lake, and to report thereon to the House'. He had at first intended to propose an Address calling for Lake to be prosecuted by the Attorney General for murder, but as no remains of the man had been found and while there was some doubt as to his death, he thought the House would be unlikely to direct a prosecution where a true bill would not be found.[8]

Although he disclaimed any intention of aggravating the case by 'high colouring', one quotation - supposedly verbatim - suggests that by modern standards his oratory fell into precisely that style. Two small samples will be enough,[9] 'The seaman who had fought and bled in the cause of the country, must not be left to the mercy of every petty tyrant; must not be delivered up to the caprice of a man who will be capricious because he has the power to do so. The blood of a fellow subject and a fellow man, must not be wasted away at the pleasure of a remorseless and unpitying authority...'

And later, 'It was to a death like this that he was consigned; a lingering detail of all the suffering that can be laid upon our nature, when the pains of a body burning under a tropical sun, were wound up by the bitter depression of a mind that was never to hear the sound of a human voice again - never to feel the consolation of a human presence, but sink from hour to hour, helpless, hopeless, deserted and in despair.'

Burdett said his attention had first been called to the Sombrero incident by a newspaper paragraph saying that a seaman had been left on the island by Captain Lake. Unfortunately Sir Francis did not mention the name of the newspaper or the date, but he said that the incident seemed to have been regarded as trivial 'like a common occurrence of the day, such as 'a stage coach was overturned in Piccadilly, but we are happy to say that none of the passengers were hurt'.

Notwithstanding all that had now been done, he felt something further was necessary. The various allegations made by Charles Thomas should be investigated. One of the facts (the landing of Robert Jeffery) had been proved, and there was every reason to give credit to the rest.

Sir Francis 'rather thought that the man must have perished upon the island', but whether he had or not the moral guilt of this 'unexampled act of oppression' was the same. Uninhibited by any question of prejudicing a future trial, he added that the evidence of the principal witnesses at the court martial, Spencer and Hobson, had virtually shown them to be accomplices in the act. He suggested that there was a conspiracy to get rid of Jeffery. When the master replied to a question from Lake that there were two thieves on board, Captain Lake had said 'Send up Jeffery', and told him he would not keep such a fellow on board his ship. Spencer had also admitted that he had often said to Lake that it would be a very good thing if they could get Jeffery out of the ship: that flogging would do him no good. They themselves must have expected Jeffery to perish for they had robbed him of his clothes and money, and supplied him with neither food nor water.

Burdett next referred to the 'curious and ineffectual but imperfect search for the body' which had been made two months afterwards and condemned Admiral Cochrane's 'indifference'. As to those who made the search, it was shocking that 'at a moment when they were to ascertain the life or death of one human being, and perhaps, to decide upon the life and death of another, they should be so little impressed with the dreadful duty in which they were occupied as to turn it into a party of pleasure and divide their time between searching for the body and shooting at wild birds'.

All the persons concerned in the search should have been called to give evidence or, if any selection were to be made, those who had concurred in landing Jeffery should have been the last to be chosen. The statement that no traces of the man were found rested on Spencer's evidence alone; not a single question had been put on this point to Hobson, the only other witness at the court martial who had been with Spencer in the search.

The admiral had represented the island as 'so near and convenient', yet the distance between Anegada and Sombrero was seven or eight leagues (21-24 miles - still a considerable underestimate). Even if Lake had been insane or in liquor when he ordered Jeffery to be landed, this excuse could hardly have served for his neglect to take him off next day.

One of the witnesses had said 'he had heard, from one who had heard from another, that an account appeared in one of the American papers, stating, that he was taken away by a vessel which touched at the island'. Even if such a statement had appeared this defence was absurd, said Sir Francis, who had no great opinion of the press - at least in England, where papers were 'apt to kill and to bring to life without much foundation'.

Spencer had said that neither he nor Lake had thought Sombrero a desolate island when they landed Jeffery. Yet Lieutenant Mould and others climbed the rocks to see whether it was inhabited, and on their return said it was not. Burdett repeated his inference that there was a conspiracy between Spencer and Lake to get rid of Jeffery, and 'it would have been more merciful if they had thrown him into the sea'. It was impossible that anyone would think the island was inhabited, said Burdett, quoting from 'Brookes and other gazetteers', all of which described Sombrero as barren and desolate. If Captain Lake was sincere when he said he would give £20,000 rather than have left Jeffery on Sombrero, he should have spent part of it on inquiries in America as to his fate.

The defence made by Lake before the court martial was as unsatisfactory as the evidence was conclusive against him, Sir Francis went on. It was strange that such an act as he had committed should be punished only with admonition and dismissal from the service. All the world must agree that he was guilty. The court martial had not pushed home many important questions; there appeared to have been a desire merely to take off the edge of public indignation.

The next speaker was Prime Minister Spencer Perceval (Northampton), confusingly referred to in Hansard as the chancellor of the exchequer, an office which (remarkable as it seems to us) he also held, five others having refused it. He was also chancellor of the Duchy of Lancaster. Perceval was a lawyer, a former attorney general. He had been prime minister for only two months, and his political situation was critical, mainly because of England's lack of success in the war with Napoleon, of which the disastrous Scheldt expedition was the most recent example. Perceval was determined to carry on the war but his ministry was regarded as weak, and his own back-benchers were all too apt to rebel. Scandals like the Jeffery case were an embarrassment.

So the prime minister, 'a short, fair, pale-faced' man[10], trod a delicate path. He did not attempt to deny the importance of the case, and agreed that it was no excuse for Lake to allege that he did not know the island was uninhabited. However, as befitted a senior lawyer, he looked at the legal points arising. He gave his opinion that the court martial sentence would not prevent Lake being tried for murder, but that there was no evidence against the captain except what bore on the point for which he had been punished, equivalent to an assault with intent to murder. It was no slight punishment for him to be 'broke' by a court martial. If a committee would have no power to direct any further proceedings, what practical good would it do to appoint one?

There was no conclusive evidence to show whether Jeffery was dead or alive; and the idea that he was safe, Perceval claimed, was grounded on evidence other than the paragraph in the American paper, without revealing what it might be. There was no point in the House ordering Lake to be indicted for murder without proof that Jeffery was dead. Lake would then only be acquitted, in which case he could not be tried again if a body were subsequently found.[11]

Perceval sensibly suggested it would be better to wait to see whether by additional enquiries any further information could be obtained. Then, if Jeffery were found to have died as a result of having been left on the island, a trial might be ordered. He also pointed out, lawyer-like, that if Jeffery were alive, he could sue Lake for damages. As to Thomas's allegations of frauds, this subject was being investigated.

The prime minister invited Burdett to withdraw his motion for the present, and threatened that if this were not done he would vote against it. However it should not be supposed that the House thought lightly of the case, or that they dissented from the motion for any reason other than that there was insufficient evidence to order a prosecution for murder.

It was now the turn of Samuel Whitbread (Bedford). Only a month before he had mounted a hugely successful attack on Chatham for the failure of the Scheldt operation and five years earlier had led a move to impeach Lord Melville, Treasurer of the Navy, following disclosure of abuses in that department, though in the event Melville was acquitted.

Backing his friend Sir Francis Burdett in what seems to have been a moderate speech, Whitbread reminded the government that the motion went further than the case of Captain Lake. What had the Admiralty done about Admiral Sir Alexander Cochrane, who was 'deeply accountable'? Knowing about the Sombrero incident, he had allowed Lake to be promoted; the Admiralty should order some proceedings against him. As for Lake, the sentence was very lenient, but could he be still tried for murder on the evidence before the House? Whitbread said that if he were a grand juror he would have to say 'no true bill', and if he were a petty juror he would have to say 'not guilty'. But other witnesses should be examined, particularly Lieutenant Mould and Mr Windsor, who joined the *Recruit* as purser after the Sombrero incident but heard of it from Spencer and others still serving.

The Admiralty, said Whitbread, should now order a more thorough search of the island for the body of this sailor. Perceval had warned that if Lake were now tried for murder and acquitted, it would be dreadful if Jeffery's body were found later with no possibility of a second trial. Whitbread put the reverse case: how much more shocking would it be if Lake were tried now and convicted of murder (which, of course, carried the death penalty), and that afterwards it should turn out that Jeffery was still alive. The House should steer clear of either possibility.

Whitbread suggested that, instead of a committee of the House being appointed, it would be better to agree upon an address to the Crown for a search to be made for Jeffery's remains, and for all means to be used to ascertain whether he be alive or not.

Several Members who had visited or served in the West Indies felt it their duty to give 'first-hand' descriptions of Sombrero. Unfortunately their memories, and their practical knowledge, were defective in various degrees. It is doubtful whether any of them had landed on the desolate island. Why should they?

James Stephen (Tralee) had practised as a barrister in the island of St Kitts, and on returning to England became a campaigner with Wilberforce against slavery. A supporter of Perceval, on this occasion he did not distinguish himself. He began his speech by stating disarmingly that he had not had time to look at the documents until he entered the chamber that night, so it was to be understood that he 'did not give any decided opinion upon the evidence produced upon the court martial'. He then proceeded to do so.

He said he had sailed close to Sombrero 'and from the glance he had of it, he could take upon himself to assure the House that it was uninhabited, and that it was impossible that any individual, cast upon it, could there find the means of subsistence'. With the knowledge that he had of its desolate situation, he - taking up Whitbread's simile - 'could have no hesitation, were he a grand juror, in finding a true bill against the person who would wantonly devote a fellow being to such a fate...' And 'if some strong evidence was not adduced in the defence, he would not hesitate, were he a petty juror upon the trial of such an offender, to bring in a verdict of murder'.

This last statement, especially for a lawyer - who in the following year was appointed a Chancery master - was going a bit far. The veteran politician and dramatist Richard Brinsley Sheridan (Ilchester), who generally approved of Stephen's views, said he was astonished at the remark, 'such a doctrine was almost as bad as any thing Captain Lake had done'. The Attorney General, Sir Vicary Gibbs (University of Cambridge), a tiny, elderly, humourless Tory, was the man who would have to set on foot any prosecution ordered by the House (the office of Director of Public Prosecutions did not then exist.) He found it necessary politely to disagree with Stephen that there was ground for a verdict of murder.

One other MP, John Christian Curwen (Carlisle), a moderate Whig, did support Stephen's attitude. He said that on the court martial evidence he would find Lake guilty of murder; it was no excuse to say he thought the island inhabited, he ought to have known. Stephen said that Sombrero was a 'bleak, sandy island, not perhaps more than twice or thrice a year trodden upon by human feet'. He had heard that it had no fresh water, and he thought it was impossible that it could have any.

The sailors in the House opposed such a poorly-founded view. Admiral Sir Eliab Harvey (Essex) said that 'justice and humanity required him to state to the House, that the island of Sombrero was a rock, and that water must lodge and be found in many of the cavities. Also the eggs of birds 'were to be had in such abundance, that no man had to perish for want of food and water'.

Captain John Poo Beresford (Coleraine) said he had been stationed 'off' Sombrero for three years, and near it for seven. He had served in fact under Admiral Duckworth in the reduction of several of the islands in the Virgins group and thought it hardly possible for a man to remain on Sombrero 24 hours, for 'if he waved his hat every morning, he must be observed'. He did not know whether the island was actually inhabited, but claimed it was 'daily' resorted to by fishermen.

Lord Folkestone (Salisbury), heir to the distinguished Whig politician the Earl of Radnor, was another MP who played a leading part in opposing abuses of the time. He now supported Whitbread's idea of an Address to promote a search for Jeffery or his remains. He also thoughtfully pointed out that, as Jeffery had not deserted, there must be an arrear of wages due to him, and this must be paid to him or, if dead, to his relatives.

The Members connected with the Admiralty or the navy knew they could not condone the Sombrero incident but, not unexpectedly, did everything else possible to mitigate its effects.

John Wilson Croker (Downpatrick), an Irish lawyer who had been made Secretary of the Admiralty as a reward for his services to the party, was of course a Perceval supporter. He answered criticisms made by Burdett about the witnesses called at the court martial. Lieutenant Mould, he said, had gone to the East Indies, and the Admiralty did not think it advisable to delay the court martial until his return 'which could not be expected in less than a year'. (Had he been brought back specially, it could surely have been done in a shorter time.) Mr Windsor had not come to the *Recruit* until a year after the incident which he and almost everyone else referred to as 'this transaction'.

Sheridan, after rebuking the lawyer James Stephen for his prejudiced remarks, told the House that he (Sheridan) had some information collected by Captain Lake's friends which induced him to believe that Lake did not know the island was uninhabited. It appeared from this that many of the ship's officers did not think the island uninhabited. He backed the call for a search and inquiry to discover Jeffery, and disclosed that Lake's family had been, and still were, making strenuous efforts to find out whether Jeffery had been taken off by an American vessel, and if he were yet alive. Sheridan backed the idea of a committee, and remarked that it should also report on the conduct of Admiral Cochrane who could never have regarded Lake as capable of leaving a man on a desolate island otherwise he would have court-martialled him then and there.

Admiral Sir Richard Bickerton (Poole), a Lord of the

Admiralty and married to the daughter of an Antiguan doctor, was defensive. It was not true that the Admiralty had appointed Lake to a ship after receiving Cochrane's report on the case. As for Jeffery's property 'it was impossible, from the rules of the navy' that any man could be cheated of what belonged to him. He also defended Cochrane's conduct as based on the supposition that Jeffery had safely reached America.

The other Lord of the Admiralty present, Robert Plumer Ward (Haslemere), also a lawyer, was brother-in-law to Lord Mulgrave the First Lord. He praised Cochrane highly as 'one of the best officers in the British service'; the Admiralty were satisfied with his conduct after the explanation they had received and he thought there was no need to inquire further, a view shared by the Attorney General.

One more naval officer had yet to speak: Captain Lord Cochrane (Honiton), who spoke generously in favour of his uncle, Sir Alexander. The admiral, he said, had acted too leniently 'which was his known character'. However, he had sent Lake home to be tried where he was sure justice would be done. Lord Cochrane said he had no doubt that when the matter came to be inquired into by a committee Sir Alexander's character would 'appear in the fairest light', and the whole world would be convinced that he had conducted himself 'as became an admiral of the British navy'.

George Canning, MP for Wendover and former Foreign Secretary, was a supporter of Perceval, although he would not take an appointment under him. He had been Secretary at War at the time of the Scheldt disaster and did not intend to be implicated again.

He now suggested that no Member could be certain either as to the risk run by Jeffery or the knowledge which Lake possessed concerning the island but it was necessary to find out as soon as possible the truth of these matters. If Jeffery had been saved, he thought no more need be done; if he were dead, further steps would be needed 'for the sake of justice'.

An Address for an inquiry was the correct course.

Sir Francis Burdett intervened at this point. He reminded the House of the opinion of the ship's crew, that Jeffery had been left to starve and die on the island. If Lake could not be prosecuted for murder, he hoped they would punish him in another way, by bringing an action for his illegal taking of Jeffery's clothes (which had been sold to the crew), as was often done in cases of child-stealing where the greater offence escaped punishment. He believed that a man could be tried in the civil courts after having been tried by martial law 'otherwise he might, for an offence against the law, be rescued from the law by a military court'.

Sir Francis then bowed to the general view that a Crown inquiry would be more effective than a Commons committee and withdrew his motion.

Whitbread had already drawn up an alternative motion calling for a fresh search to be made of the island, this time by two commissioners.

The debate then resumed, with Whitbread pointing out the conflict between the description of Sombrero given by the impulsive James Stephen, the lawyer who had practised in St Kitts, 'a low sandy island, in which there was neither food nor water' - and the rather more hospitable place it appeared from the MPs acquainted with it as officers who had mentioned cavities filled with rainwater and many birds' eggs.

Stephen took this as a reflection on his truthfulness, and said he had not made the unqualified statement attributed to him. He became so hot under the collar that the Speaker had to intervene. Whitbread ended the storm by saying he had not meant to question Stephen's veracity. The troubled waters were further calmed by Sir Charles Hamilton (Honiton), yet another naval officer with West Indian experience. He said that the island appeared as Stephen had announced when seen from a distance but in fact there were plenty of shell-fish, birds and eggs on which a man might live a long time.

Nevertheless every officer, he said, must be ashamed of Lake's conduct.

The prime minister said he did not suppose that it was necessary to send two commissioners to the West Indies, to walk over an island a mile and a half in circumference, and only half a mile long. The Admiralty could make the inquiry.

The next speaker was Sir John Sinclair, the great agriculturist and statistician. A Scotsman, he happened to sit for the Cornish rotten borough of Lostwithiel, but his intervention now was the result of a complete accident.

While the debate on Jeffery continued, he had chanced (perhaps having returned to the chamber after a brief absence) to sit under the gallery of the House.[12] An American businessman had been given a seat there as a visitor, and told Sinclair that he had received a letter by the last packet from New York, stating that Jeffery was in fact alive and safe in that city. Sir John, 'much struck with so singular a circumstance', decided he ought to mention it to the House to prevent any action being taken on the assumption that the man was dead. The American, unfortunately, did not have the letter with him.

So all Sir John could say was that he had 'good reason' to believe that Jeffery was alive and in New York, and that he supported the prime minister's view that an Admiralty inquiry would be adequate.

Hon. William Wellesley Pole (Queen's County), the former Secretary of the Admiralty and incidentally Wellington's elder brother, agreed that an inquiry was necessary, but suggested that if instructions were sent to the American Minister there would not even be need to involve the Admiralty.

The curious point had been made by Sheridan and some others that it was not unknown for naval officers to leave a man on an inhabited island. Although Wellesley Pole could not deny this, he said he must 'express his reprobation of such a practice', adding that the navy was 'not in such a state as to require any such expedients, and such assertions going abroad might prove injurious to the service'. The case of Daly v Rolles (see chapter four) must still have been fresh in the collective memory of the Admiralty and many MPs.

Mr Sheridan carefully explained that he had stated it was 'not unusual' to land men on inhabited islands, but he had never claimed men had been left on uninhabited ones.

Whitbread said the 'solemnity' of appointing commissioners to make the inquiry was 'not due in respect to the extent of the island, but to the enormity of the offence'; though he somewhat detracted from this by suggesting that if any officers were going to the West Indies, they might be appointed.

However, the Home Secretary threatened to divide the House if Whitbread did not withdraw the reference to commissioners, so he agreed, whereupon the motion was passed nem. con., 'That a humble Address be presented to His Majesty that He will be graciously pleased to give immediate directions that the most Minute and accurate search be made in the Island of Sombrero in the West Indies for the purpose of ascertaining whether any traces can there be found of Robert Jeffery a sailor late of His Majesty's Ship *Recruit* there landed contrary to every principle of Duty, and in violation of every dictate of humanity, by order of the Honourable Warwick Lake late commanding His Majesty's said ship.'

Whitbread then moved a second Address which, after minor amendments, was also passed nem. con. in the following terms, 'That a humble Address be presented to His Majesty that He will be graciously pleased to give such directions as He shall think best adapted to the circumstances of the case that diligent enquiry shall be made both within His Majesty's Dominions, on board the Royal Navy and the commercial Navy of the Country as well as in Foreign countries so far as the same shall be possible to ascertain whether Robert Jeffery a sailor late belonging to His Majesty's ship *Recruit* is now alive or has been alive at any time subsequent to December 13, 1807'.

After this Samuel Whitbread pushed things a little too far by moving a third address calling for an inquiry into the conduct of Vice-Admiral Sir Alexander Cochrane.

The prime minister said that if Whitbread were to have Cochrane court-martialled it would be carrying the feeling of the House to an extravagant length. Admiral Harvey echoed this with the specious comment that 'inconvenience to the public service' would arise from withdrawing the commanders of vessels from their ships and the commander-in-chief from his station in order to attend a court martial.

Robert Plumer Ward, a civil lord, said that Cochrane's explanation, while not justifying the Admiralty's approval had been satisfactory enough for them to abstain from any proceeding with a view to censure it. Lord Cochrane, the admiral's nephew, pointed out that Lake had been sent home on half-pay 'in consequence of his conduct' but that the lords of the Admiralty had thought proper to promote him. Admiral Sir Charles Pole (Plymouth) remarked that Cochrane ought to have stated why he had sent Lake home on half-pay.

William Wellesley Pole, who had been Secretary of the Admiralty at that time, made it clear that what Lord Cochrane had asserted was entirely new both to him and to the Admiralty which had known nothing about the Sombrero incident.

Samuel Whitbread said he would withdraw his motion for an Address calling for an inquiry into Admiral Cochrane's conduct, on an understanding that the Admiralty would call on the admiral for a further explanation. He concluded by moving that copies of all relevant papers should be laid before the House, and this was agreed.

Two days after the debate Sir Francis Burdett was arrested on a Speaker's warrant. He was taken to the Tower of London through streets guarded by thousands of soldiers and imprisoned until the end of the parliamentary session several weeks later.

Although the cause of his arrest was not connected with Jeffery's case, it illustrates how tense were relations between Government and Opposition at this moment. The warrant, which had been issued before the Sombrero debate, alleged that Burdett had committed a breach of privilege by issuing a copy of a speech which he had made in support of a radical orator.

This speech was first published in Cobbett's *Political Register*, which made many editorial attacks on the Government over the treatment of Jeffery. Two months later, in June 1810, William Cobbett himself was sentenced to two years' imprisonment and a fine of £1,000 for an article attacking flogging in the Army. His later articles on Jeffery were dated from Newgate Prison.

Chapter 7

WITNESSES GALORE

The Commons debate, coming after reports of the court martial, ensured that Robert Jeffery's case was known to every newspaper reader. It had amply fed the appetite for sensations - and the story was by no means finished yet. After all, it might even end in a murder trial, or at least a civil lawsuit in which the under-dog, in the shape of a rescued Jeffery, sued an aristocratic bully, ex-Captain Lake.

Certainly it attracted much genuine sympathy as well as the attentions of a few publicity-seekers. While official action to implement the Commons resolution took its course, a steady flow of people with real or imagined information on Jeffery's fate or whereabouts came forward. Sir Francis Burdett, whose interest had been primarily political, was now confined in the Tower where he could play little further part in the drama. He was content to leave the continuing human aspects of the case to Samuel Whitbread who nevertheless kept him informed, with copies of papers as they came to hand.[1] It was Whitbread, too, whom the irrepressible Thomas chose as the recipient of his continuing barrage of letters.

The first useful contact came in Mr Whitbread's mail only days after the Commons debate. In a letter dated April 9, a Dr Oke Millett of Hayle in Cornwall said that his brother, a Lieutenant William Millett of HMS *Aboukir*, had recently spent a few days near Polperro.[2] He was perhaps visiting another brother there for the local curate, who apparently served both parishes, Lansallos and Talland, was also named Millett.[3] The lieutenant had learned that Jeffery's friends had heard from (more likely heard of) him 'since he made his escape from the island on board an American vessel'.

The doctor suggested that Whitbread write to 'Mr Job of Polperro' or the Collector of Customs at Looe or Fowey, asking them to try to establish the truth of this story. He thoughtfully explained in a footnote that 'Polperro was a fishing cove near Looe'. (A few years earlier, when a proposal had been made to improve the postal service there, Lord Charles Spencer as joint postmaster-general had minuted drily that 'the existence of the Town of Polpero happens to be new to me'...[4]).

Dr. Millett's letter took only three days to reach Whitbread who wrote immediately to Mr Job. He, too, replied by return of post with the first 'hard' information about Robert Jeffery yet to reach anyone in authority.[5]

Zephaniah Job, a remarkable figure, was known in Cornwall as the 'smugglers' banker', and did indeed act as agent and banker for many privateers and smugglers in the French wars. However, he was also a substantial merchant and venturer, steward of two important local landowners, and by 1810 had become the respected and influential doyen of Polperro, a village which had neither resident squire nor local government and was divided between two parishes.

On receiving Whitbread's letter Job had called on Robert Jeffery's mother and 'found her in great distress', believing her son dead. She was so hard up that 'even the value of the Cloaths of her son would be an object to her'. Job then found that John Libby, one of the Polperro seamen who had been Jeffery's shipmate in the *Recruit,* was now home. Libby described the Sombrero incident, and said he was 'so shocked at the cruel treatment of his neighbour that he scarce knew what he did or what was done'. Libby revealed however that he was not in the boat with Jeffery, nor a member of the party sent back to search the island for him.

Libby told Job that when the ship returned to Barbados after the search there was a report that Jeffery had been taken off the island by a frigate 'whose name he could not recollect' and that Jeffery having eaten his own flesh 'as far as his teeth could reach' had died three days after his rescue. This story was to prove persistent and no one ever succeeded in discovering its origin. If Mrs Coad, the boy's mother, had learned of it, no wonder she was in distress. Jeffery had apparently begged one of the boat's crew to tell Libby not to let his mother know of his being abandoned on the island. Whether or not Libby had received or honoured this request the Sombrero incident by now was public knowledge.

Job added a postscript, saying that he had since found that another of the boy's shipmates from Polperro, Richard Oliver Johns, had again been pressed into the navy again, and was now on board a Plymouth-bound impress tender at Swansea. In this, apparently, Job knew more than the Admiralty which attempted to summon Johns for questioning by despatching a message to the Polperro post office. Richard Johns had said he had been a crew member of the captain's gig. Some time after Jeffery was landed, he went on, Captain Lake had boarded a certain warship where he learned that they had taken a man from Sombrero who had eaten his own flesh and died three days after being taken on board.

Shrewdly Job expressed his doubts about whether this latter story could be believed. Surely, he argued, an occurrence of that sort would have been entered in the warship's log and reported to the Admiralty.

A slightly different version appeared in *The Times* of April 19, dated Plymouth, April 16 and stated to be copied from 'an evening paper'.[6] According to this report, on the previous Friday, April 13, two smugglers 'who had been some time in the American merchant service' arrived at Fowey with a letter to Mrs. Coad from the American captain with whom they had sailed and who had stated that he took Jeffery off the island 'after he had been a fortnight without sustenance: that he had eaten the flesh off his arm, and died in two hours after having been taken on board'. Such information the captain had offered to confirm on oath.

The Plymouth reporter, or perhaps the editor of the evening paper in which it first appeared, concluded this ghoulish story, 'I shall forbear entering more fully into this business till I have made a full inquiry, and for that purpose have sent down to Fowey. In the mean time, give me leave to say that I conceive the statement rests on a good foundation'.

Whitbread sent on Job's letter to the Admiralty. The port admiral at Plymouth was instructed to despatch an officer by land to Polperro to find Libby (which he could do by enquiring of Zephaniah Job) and bring him first to Plymouth whence he was to be sent to the flagship at Spithead.[7] Richard Johns was also to be found and brought up for questioning. This proved less easy as at first no one knew where the impress tender was. Eventually it was found and orders conveyed for this man, too, to be taken to Spithead.[8]

Ben Coad, Robert Jeffery's stepfather, had naturally read or had read to him an account of the Parliamentary debate. He spotted Sir John Sinclair's reference to a report that Robert was alive and in New York, and promptly wrote to Sir John asking for further information.[9] Sinclair replied kindly, explaining that the 'news' was based on a letter sent to the American businessman whom he had met by chance in the House of Commons. Tantalisingly, the American had left unexpectedly for the Continent 'but he is soon to return & I shall lose no time in procuring from him as soon as he reaches London, an extract of the Letter.'

Coad now wrote a long letter to Samuel Whitbread. Evidently it was written or copied out for him, probably by Job, but he signed his name to it neatly enough. In it Coad passed on what Sinclair had told him which, apparently, was new to Whitbread who followed it up with a letter to Sir John.

The baronet replied on April 26 from Holkham, the Norfolk seat of Coke, where he was one of an Easter house party.[10] 'Nothing could be more positive than the declaration of the American Gentleman', he affirmed. The American went to France two or three days after the debate; Sir John had no doubt he would show Whitbread the letter or an extract from it. 'Stories of a different complexion,' Sinclair added, 'may be raised by the foes of England in America, who will take a pleasure in circulating any falsehood that can have the effect of disgusting our sailors with the naval service of their own country.' This comment may well explain some of the horror stories which were beginning to appear. However, of the American gentleman and his letter there was not another word.

Ben Coad's main object in writing to Whitbread had been to plead his own case. He would not presume to describe his wife's anguish at 'the horrid transaction what I call inhuman murder', or his own feelings 'as the Boy was as naturel as my own & had brought him to work at my trade with me'. However, by the time he had married the widowed Mrs. Jeffery and bought the plot on which to build a house and workshop, he had no money left and fell into debt. Robert having been made a 'life' on the lease Coad would lose one-third of his security if the boy had died.[11]

Coad reported that he had written to Sir Francis Burdett asking whether some compensation might be expected: his circumstances including 'the failure of trade' meant that he could not afford to sue Lake. Evidently Burdett could not have received the letter and was now, of course, imprisoned in the Tower, so Coad asked Whitbread's view.

The official search for Jeffery ordered by the House of Commons had to be set on foot as quickly as possible. Mr Secretary Richard Ryder (the Home Secretary, we should term him) had written formally to the Admiralty on April 10 with copies of the resolutions.[12] However, one thing was surprisingly lacking - any physical description of Jeffery. Whitbread again called upon the help of Mr Job, who replied on Easter Saturday, April 21, 'I have as you desired applied to the Mother of Robt Jeffery for his description: He was 18 years of age the 11 Decr 1807, two days before he was landed on the Island, about 5 feet 7 inches high, slight made at that time, Oval face, rather a long visage - very light hair & Eye-brows

- Grey Eyes - his Left knee bent a little inwards.

'His mother saith that he was bred a Blacksmith & worked at the trade four or five years & was a good tradesman. That his Life was on the Cottage & Shop where she liveth & wch is held on lease under John Phillipps Carpenter Esqr so that his death will be a material loss to her.'[13]

A printed document, dated April 11 (the day after the Admiralty had received official copies of the Addresses from Secretary Ryder) had already been prepared calling on officers to make all possible enquiries to discover out Jeffery's whereabouts. Job's description of Jeffery was now added on a separate printed sheet.

The Admiralty had also requested a description of Jeffery from Edward Spencer, formerly master of the *Recruit*, and now serving in HMS *Iris*. Spencer's reply was not written until May 21, much too late for the circular. It reflected the way he had regarded 18-year-old Robert, at the time of the marooning, describing the young man as 'apparently about 21 years of age' and, '...fair but of a sickly hue ... his person generally was of a weakly appearance judging from its being rather very speare (spare) and emaciated - this however seemed to be his natural habit of body.'[14]

The notice was widely distributed, in particular to the 'regulating captains' in charge of the impress service at the principal ports. Inquiries in America would mainly be the concern of the Foreign Office. Whether because of these instructions, or simply from the sensational publicity, men who claimed to know something of Jeffery, or even to have met him, came forward one after the other.

On April 24 a former *Recruit* seaman named William Watt was discovered - or came forward - at Dundee, in Scotland. He had been invalided out of the navy and was now a weaver. The local regulating captain hauled him before the Provost of Dundee to swear a statement.[15] This produced another variation on the story of Jeffery's escape.

Watt said (gratuitously or in answer to an officious question, for it can hardly have mattered now) that Jeffery's 'general character' was bad. Coad added that the week after the Sombrero incident (in fact it was a month) the brig boarded the *Mary Ann* of Liverpool en route from Africa to Jamaica. The Guineaman was found to have more than her permitted number of slaves, so Lake seized her and sent her into Barbados with one of his officers and ten men, of whom Watt was one, taking a dozen of the crew in exchange.

In Barbados, Watt took the opportunity to desert. During his stay of about a month on the island, he met a man he called 'Jefferson' who told him that he had stayed 12 or 13 days on Sombrero, subsisting chiefly on fruit and rainwater. He gave Watt to understand that he intended to go to Philadelphia, 'for the purpose of working at his profession as an Armourer as he expected more encouragement than here in his own Country'.

A few days after this meeting the deserter Watt was impressed by a boat's crew from HMS *Pelican*. Under the assumed name of William Craig he served three months in her before being sent to hospital in Jamaica with a leg injury he sustained at the taking of the island of Deseada. From there he was sent home to Portsmouth's Haslar Hospital and in due course discharged.

The account which Watt gave could have been true if the American schooner which rescued Jeffery had put in to Barbados. However, Watt could not have met him there earlier than the third week in January 1808, about the time when, according to Jeffery's own account, the schooner actually reached Marblehead. Even if the timing could be reconciled, Jeffery, in an otherwise detailed narrative, makes no mention of visiting Barbados. Indeed it seems highly unlikely that he would have risked being found in a port frequented by British warships including the *Recruit*.

On April 25, the day after Watt's appearance, a much better witness turned up in Liverpool when George Hassell, a 25-

year-old sailor from Marblehead itself, chanced to be in port. On Easter Sunday he happened to pick up the previous day's paper, the Liverpool *Saturday's Advertizer*. Reading that orders had been received at Plymouth on the previous Thursday for a 'Swift sailing Cutter to prepare to sail for America and from thence to the Island of Sombrero and all the other West India Islands to search for and endeavour to ascertain the fate of Jeffrey the Seaman', Hassell decided to come forward so that Jeffery's friends might know where he was.

He was questioned, and swore a statement before the Mayor of Liverpool, John Clarke.[16] His account, supported by circumstantial detail, reported that two or three days before he left the towns of Marblehead and Beverly in March 1809, he met 'a Person of the Name of Jeffrey who he understood was by a Trade a Blacksmith' and who told him that he had been put ashore on Sombrero. There followed a substantially correct version of what followed, judged by Jeffery's own later story as well as by the court martial evidence. It was mistaken in two points only. One was the length of time Jeffery had remained on the island before being rescued, which Hassell put at 'three or four days'. The other was that the Marblehead schooner which effected the rescue was the *Betsey*, Captain Francis, rather than the *Adams*, Captain Dennis.[17] In the context these were comparatively unimportant details.

Hassell said he took Jeffery to be aged about 22 or 23, about five feet four or five inches tall with a light complexion and rather slender build. Jeffery told him that while on Sombrero he had subsisted upon crabs, and had drunk rainwater from the rock crevices. After his rescue he had first lived with a Marblehead butcher, then went to Beverley and worked for a blacksmith, from whom - Hassell understood - he received 18 dollars a month. He was well known in the neighbourhood of Marblehead and went by his own name, though he 'was generally called by the Name of the Governor of Sombrero it being so notoriously known there that he had been put on shore by the orders of the Captain of an English Sloop of War'. Marblehead people had suspected Jeffery guilty of something serious, until Hassell met a deserter from the *Recruit* on board another ship, who told him that the theft of spruce beer was the reason for Jeffery's punishment.

No mention here of Jeffery having been at Barbados, no suggestion of the ghoulish 'flesh-eating'. Later Hassell's account was to prove useful in tracing young Robert's whereabouts in America.

The lurid versions did not disappear easily, and until Jeffery was found could not be disproved. Lieutenant William Millett of HMS *Aboukir* who was still at Lansallos wrote to his brother the doctor on April 28 with some further details from Lieutenant Mould (a Fowey man) and John Libby, Jeffery's shipmate, which Millett had picked up, probably at second hand.[18]

'Libby supposes that when he (Jeffery) found famine would put a dreadful period to his life, to avoid the pangs of famine, he cast himself into the sea'. It was implied that Lake had given the order to land Jeffery after dining well in the wardroom, and that he usually 'drank freely'. Before sending the letter to Whitbread, Dr. Millett struck out the words 'He was a complete tyrant, at all times', on the ground that such a statement based only on hearsay should not be included. Lieutenant Millett, who of course did not know about the recent witnesses, Watt and Hassell, said that the reports of Jeffery's escape to America could be traced to no specific author. 'I sometimes think,' Millett went on, 'that the report was put about by Lake's friends.' Nor, however, could an author be found for the report that any American or any English ship of war took him off the island, 'with his arms stripped of flesh, to their bones - and that death ensued three hours afterwards'. Jeffery's mother and uncle (presumably he meant 'step-father') had never heard directly from him, and if he had survived surely an official account would have reached the government, if not his mother.

A man named John Marley, who had served as a Royal Marine in the *Recruit*, was another who recounted the flesh-eating version of the story. Like Watt, he had been invalided and now lived at the Britannia pub opposite the Royal Marine barracks at Woolwich where doubtless after a pint he told his tale time and again to his cronies or gullible new recruits.

He related the now well-known facts of Jeffery's landing and of the subsequent search-and-shooting parties from the brig. Marley claimed that the men despatched on shore did not know until they returned that the object of their visit had been to look for Jeffery, which gives them little credit for common sense.

Marine Marley embellished his story with an account of his own alleged sufferings on board the *Recruit*. He said he had been ship's corporal but was reduced to the ranks for saying that the landing of Jeffery was 'a pity, and a shocking thing, and that if it was known in England Captain Lake would get worked for it'. Midshipman Graham, who had reported Jeffery for taking the spruce beer, overheard Marley's remark and reported it to Lake.

After that his story strains our credulity. According to Marley the captain had him seized, carried aft to the poop, put in double irons and gagged with an iron-handled hammer. Lake then went below and brought up a pistol, loaded it with ball cartridge, and declared: 'You damned rascal, I'll blow your brains out'. According to Marley, Captain Lake rammed a pistol into his ears, making them bleed, then struck him on the head with the butt. Marley, so he said, remained on the poop in irons for three weeks and four days, and was then given four dozen lashes and reduced to the ranks.

At Antigua on August 16, 1808 (by which time Lake had left the ship) some marines serving in a frigate named HMS *Blonde* told Marley that the captain of an American fishing boat which had called at Sombrero for salt had told the *Blonde*'s captain that he had taken from that island a seaman belonging to the *Recruit*. The American had reported 'that (this man) was in a starving and dying state; that the Flesh of his Arm was torn; they discovered him by observing a piece of an Old Check shirt tied to a stick close to the place where he was found;

100

that he lived only a few hours after he got on board the said American vessel, when his body was buried in the usual way by launching it over board.'

Marley himself was invalided at Antigua. The notes of his replies to questions put to him in London are bound up with the court martial minutes, but are undated. They are minuted by John Barrow, the permanent Secretary of the Admiralty, to the effect that there was no indication of any such event in the log of the *Blonde*, nor any indication in Lake's log of Marley having been punished and reduced. 'But,' Mr Barrow added, 'this will be cleared up when Lieutenant Higgins (who may daily be expected) arrives in town'.

The *Recruit*'s muster book shows Marley having been reduced to the ranks in September, 1807, three months before Jeffery was landed, and reinstated the following May.[19] As to Lieutenant Higgins, the first lieutenant, now serving in the *Badger*, there was another mystery. Throughout the investigations and trial he had remained a shadowy figure. On April 17 Samuel Whitbread received a note from an informant called Barns, telling him that Higgins had kept a copy of his own log, which was now 'sealed up together with other papers' and in the custody of the lieutenant's sister, a Mrs Gill, who lived near Holborn. She also possessed one or more letters from her brother concerning the Jeffery case. Whitbread asked, through Barns, to see the letters, but apparently the lady's husband now refused permission.

Whitbread replied that he would tell the Admiralty with whom, as well as with Burdett, he shared his information on the case. It was evidently now thought worthwhile to bring Lieutenant Higgins back for questioning. Bound with the manuscript minutes of the court martial is a list of items 'to be printed', including the examinations of William Watt the *Recruit* seaman and George Hassell the Marblehead sailor. Four items listed are not among the papers bound in: examinations of Lieutenant Higgins, and the two *Recruit* seamen from Polperro, John Libby and Richard Oliver Johns, and a letter from Barrow, permanent Secretary of the Admiralty, to 'Lord

Willerby'. These items have eluded my searches, and the examination of Higgins probably never existed.

There is no indication that Lieutenant Higgins had returned to Britain before the captain of the *Badger* wrote to the Admiralty on August 15 from Heligoland asking for a new lieutenant because Higgins had 'unfortunately' been drowned when a boat was upset.[20]

Marley's story, or something quite like it, was published in at least one London newspaper. The editor of a Truro newspaper read this and asked a friend at Fowey to make inquiries of Jeffery's aunt, Mrs Anne Line, who lived there.[21] She had heard the account of the landing from Libby and Johns soon after they had been discharged and returned to Polperro, 'but these men will not say any thing about it now, as this woman says'; and she herself had nothing more to relate apart from the following anecdote.

Lieutenant Mould had left the *Recruit* at the same time as Lake, though he transferred at once to another ship, the *Nimrod*, as lieutenant.[22] When they parted, Lake said to him, 'I hope when I have another ship, we shall sail together'. Mould replied 'No never. Recollect Jeffery'. To which Lake replied, 'I wish I had never done it'.

This at least was Mould's account which evidently he told Mrs Line when he came on leave. The *Nimrod* paid off at Woolwich on 11 October, 1808, and on December 15 Mould joined the *St Alban's* bound to the East Indies and China with a convoy.

John Libby was certainly questioned thoroughly. He had settled down as a fisherman at Polperro where a lieutenant was sent with a chaise to bring him to Plymouth. He was put on board the gun-brig *Encounter* bound for Portsmouth, where he was examined by Admiral Sir Roger Curtis. Curtis then sent him up in charge of a master's mate from the flagship *Royal William* to the Admiralty, who questioned him further on two successive days, early in May 1810. Libby was away from home three weeks altogether, and put in a bill for his expenses which he took the precaution of having verified by the ubiquitous Zephaniah Job.[23]

Libby had put on new clothes to go before the mighty ones, but the coastal trip in a small ship brought his efforts to nought. So included in his bill, as well as five shillings a day in compensation for his absence from his family and job, was a sum for 'a new set of Cloaths spoiled by my long continuance in the Gun Brig - and for which I humbly hope the Honble Lord will allow me £2 10s 0, which I am justified in saying is less than my loss thereof.' Seldom can their Lordships have been asked to compensate a lower deck man for getting his clothes dirty in a warship. They paid the bill all but five shillings, which was no doubt knocked off on principle.

Richard Oliver Johns, when the tender in which he was confined as an impressed man was found, was likewise sent by Admiral Curtis from Portsmouth to the Admiralty, in the care of a master's mate from the flagship *Royal William*.

Once the court martial was over, it is difficult to see what the authorities expected to gain from these two men. It must have been clear that they had no knowledge of Jeffery's fate - unless anyone accepted Captain Lake's suggestion that Jeffery had now gone into hiding with the privateers until he could sue Lake for damages.

What had happened all this time to the egregious Charles Morgan Thomas? After 'disappearing' at the beginning of January, he suddenly wrote to the Admiralty again on March 12, this time from Bristol.[24] He announced that he had conveyed 'the Intelligence he possessed' to the 'body corporate of London' and to a Member of Parliament. He wrote once more, on March 28, to say he could not go to Plymouth to collect his wages whereupon the Navy Board patiently sent him bills on the Bristol Collector of Customs.[25]

The 'Member of Parliament' must have been Samuel Whitbread. The name of Charles Morgan Thomas had become known to every newspaper reader. The result of the Sombrero court martial had proved him to be - as he saw it - a public benefactor, yet far from being thanked he had been thrown out of employment by the Admiralty.

Direct approach to the Admiralty having failed, on April 24 he wrote one of his usual florid letters to Whitbread.[26] He assured the MP that he had never met Captain Lake and had no personal motive for bringing him to justice. He had done it as 'an Englishman and a Christian'. Now he was 'struggling with dire distress, and with the most poignant anguish of mind'. No gentleman in Bristol, where he lived, would employ a 'discarded naval officer'. Could Whitbread advise him? He had information which 'bad as the times are, will still furnish matter of astonishment', he added, possibly as an inducement.

On April 26 Whitbread wrote to the Admiralty to elicit the background to this strange correspondent who had latched on to him. The Admiralty by now had Mr Thomas's history at their finger tips and sent a long report on his activities, together with copies of Cochrane's original report on Thomas with examples of his 'itch for writing'.[27] With praiseworthy forbearance, Mr Barrow, who held the office we now call permanent secretary, left it to Whitbread to draw his own conclusions.

He did, however, add, 'I am also directed to observe that as Thomas has no other knowledge nor authority of what he has thought proper to state respecting the transaction of landing Jeffery on the Island of Sombrero than mere hearsay, their Lordships do not conceive that his presence in Town can in any shape further the object of the examination intended to be held on the several persons who were actually belonging to the *Recruit* at the time.'

On 16 April the Admiralty had laid before the House of Commons, as ordered in the debate, copies of correspondence with Admiral Sir Alexander Cochrane, including the notable letter of August 4, 1809 in which he gave his account of Thomas, his past history and his writing itch. The documents were published in a number of papers, including those in Bristol, Thomas's home town where he now lived.[28]

It could hardly be expected that this inveterate letter-writer would not defend himself in print. After taking time to send a draft pamphlet of allegations to Whitbread, and thank him for a 'condescending and consolatory letter'[29], he sat himself down to write a splendidly sarcastic letter for publication.[30] He went through the allegations seriatim, beginning with his appearance in Barbados, when - he said - he was not in want of food or clothing, but 'money and friends I did perhaps stand in need of. Admitting even your statement to be true, is Poverty a Sin?' He corrected the Admiral's account in minor details. The admiral had said he pestered him with letters. 'You might as well say that the enemy pestered you with vessels'.

The name of a certain Captain Coombe mentioned by Cochrane brought to mind an allegation he had forgotten. This captain had cruelly punished a marine but the admiral's court of inquiry had found the action justified. Instead of sending 'garbled' extracts from his letters, why had not Cochrane sent them in full? Even the admiral's leniency was held against him; reference had been made in a document to the possibility of a court martial on Thomas, and there had been talk of the Victualling Board taking action against him. Yet neither of these things had occurred. So, the inference was, Thomas could not be 'unfit for an officer' as Cochrane had made out.

In a final flourish, this curious man wrote, 'You are, indeed, Sir Alexander, like a child, 'carried away with every wind of doctrine by the sleight of men, and cunning, craftiness, whereby they lie in wait to deceive.' I had determined to say much more, but shall reserve my next fire till we are fairly brought to at the bar of the House of Commons - a consummation most heartily prayed for by, Sir, your truly obliged, if not very obedient Servant...'

What he meant by the reference to the bar of the Commons is hard to understand. Jeffery's fate was no longer uppermost in his mind. His own misfortunes, which were, had not yet come to an end.

Meanwhile Whitbread, having now seen the extraordinary letter which Thomas had written to Cochrane in the West Indies and subsequently (though too late) retracted, wrote to ask the ex-purser for an explanation. This produced another dissertation on May 8.[31] Thomas said he had been warned that the notorious letter might cause him to be punished for mutiny, although it was unofficial and sent to Cochrane 'in his private capacity as a Gentleman'. And so on.

Whitbread also asked Thomas whether it was true that he was in default with his purser's accounts. The reply was that 'some' of his accounts for the *Heureux*, his first ship, were at Barbados. As for the second, the *Demerary*, he kept no accounts of his own, but the captain's 'as far as they were made up, were correct'. The captain's cabin was the only place fit to write in, and not even there when it rained, so sieve-like was the vessel.

On May 28, 1810 Thomas wrote to Whitbread that his recent 18-day silence was due to eye trouble.[32] While Whitbread continued to correspond with him he 'had every consideration', but 'since that had ceased I have been increasingly sorrowful'. He enclosed his discharge certificate from the hospital to show that no reason had been given, and begged the MP to try to get him some part of the pay due to him, or some compensation for the 'hardships he had undergone'.

Of more interest to us, he also made a new allegation, that James Hobson, the Clerk, had committed perjury. In his usual maddening way, Thomas added, 'I would enter into particulars but my Eyes are now far from being well'. It does not appear that he ever did disclose the nature of this accusation.

Whitbread was remarkably patient with him, and on June

8 Thomas wrote with more allegations, unconnected with Jeffery, and thanked the MP for the 'civil things' contained in his letter of April 21.[33]

Chapter 8

SOMBRERO RE-VISITED

The chain of events set in motion by the Parliamentary debate progressed slowly. The Commons resolutions were received by the Admiralty on April 11, 1810 and instructions were given immediately that Admiral Sir Alexander Cochrane (Leeward Islands) and Admiral Sir John Borlase Warren (North America) should be ordered to put them into effect.[1]

Cochrane was given special orders to direct two captains to make a survey of Sombrero. This, of course, was to eliminate any possibility that Jeffery had perished there. It was to result in reports on the natural history of this tiny Caribbean island which, although unscientific, are interesting because of their early date; and in an accurate geographical and hydrographical survey on which the Admiralty based a chart of the island published in 1815.

As usual some six weeks elapsed before orders from London were put into effect by Cochrane in the West Indies. On May 31 he wrote to Captain Hayes of HMS *Freija* giving him detailed instructions. He was to take under his orders Captain Whinyates, commander of the sloop *Frolic*.[2] They were both to land on Sombrero, and jointly superintend a strict search for any traces of Robert Jeffery. The search was to be made by two lieutenants and the master from *Freija* and one lieutenant and the master of *Frolic*, each with a party of 'six steady seamen'.

Each officer was to make a separate report, including what he or his party might find in the form of food and water, and giving their opinion whether a human being could exist on the island and for how long. In addition Captain Hayes was to cause as accurate a survey of the island as possible to be made, and to note the number of vessels which passed near enough to see a person wave or make signals. Having prepared a full report, he was to return to join the admiral at the Saintes or wherever he might be.

Finally, Cochrane told Hayes that Lieutenant Salmond of the *Freija* when a midshipman had been in the boat from HMS *Recruit* that landed Jeffery. He was to be ordered to point out the spot where the man was left on shore.

The two warships, *Freija* and *Frolic* set off on Friday, June 9, took on water at Sea Cow Bay, Tortola, and after a slow journey because of a westerly current, anchored off Sombrero on the following Wednesday evening. A thorough search was mounted next day, Thursday, June 15, and on the Sunday Captain Hayes wrote his report to the admiral.[3] In addition to the formal searches ordered, two other parties of no less than 50 men each, with most of the officers, were landed. They discovered nothing more than was included in the separate reports submitted by the designated officers.

Captain Hayes said that in his view, out of the number of vessels which passed the island, there were two naval brigs, a sloop, a schooner and an American ship which came near enough to observe through a glass a person on the shore wave, or make signals. The birds were so numerous that the people killed several of them with sticks and stones.

'I am perfectly satisfied,' he concluded, 'that ...Robert Jeffery has been taken off the Island, for had he unfortunately Perished on it, it is scarcely possible, after the search we have made, that his remains should continue undiscovered'. He did not know it, but while the search was afoot further evidence had come to light that Jeffery had in fact gone to America. The time lag in communications was such that in giving an account of these events there is a constant temptation to overwork the word 'meanwhile'.

The note written by Hayes in the margin of his draft chart of the island is succinct and precise, 'The Island is flat, extremely rugged, and without Soil, except a little in a small patch near the centre on which is a little Grass, some Weeds, and a kind of Samphire, but there is nothing growing above a foot high, except two or three prickly pear plants; It abounds in a vegetable substance growing out of the Rocks, in form and size very similar to a melon, but it is covered with Prickles, and has a salt taste.

'The Island is overrun by Lizards, perfectly Black, and about sixteen inches in length; there are also some Land Crabs, and Shell Fish; and the Sea Birds frequent it by thousands, depositing their eggs in the Breeding Season, in the holes of the Rocks; but there is no fresh Water in any part of it - After a fall of Rain the Crevices in the Rocks will of course contain some, but it is soon evaporated.

'There are very regular soundings all round; and good Anchorage, on the Western shore, there being six or seven fathoms close to the Rocks, and not more than 18 or 23 miles off - There is no Beach of any description, or any place where Turtle can get on Shore.

'The Melocactus, Great Melon Thistle, or Turk's Cap; the inside is of a greenish fleshy substance, very full of Moisture; the Fruit is produced in Circles round the upper part of the Cap, of which the Black Lizards appear to be particularly fond.'

Had he realised it, Jeffery could have sliced open the prickly pear cacti and gained a little moisture and nourishment that way, though the nearly invisible spines represented a considerable hazard. The individual parties reported few items not covered by the captain's comprehensive note just quoted, though they were - as ordered - specific in detail. As regards fauna, edible or not, young birds were noted at the north end of the island, and periwinkles, whelks and 'a few' sea crabs were reported. One lieutenant was sensible enough to mention that birds' eggs were likely to be present 'in the summer months only'.

No fresh water was found, though one party came across about four gallons of brackish water which, said the officer in charge, 'I conceive a man might drink'. Several ponds of salt water and deposits of salt were found: one officer observed that in a hurricane it was likely the sea broke over a great part of the island.

The parties were, of course, particularly told to look for any traces of a human being on the island. What they found were quite minor items, mostly suggestive of the occasional visit by fishermen: human excrement, a piece of lead, some fir staves apparently cut by a knife, the traces of fires, the greater part of a pair of shoes, in pieces, and the bung of a cask.

Estimates of how long a human being could exist on Sombrero varied. Of the five officers in charge of search parties, three suggested a week or ten days as the maximum, assuming the man to find shellfish and some water. The lack of water led the other two officers to set a limit of three days. Lieutenant Meech of the *Freija* feelingly wrote, 'I think no Person could exist on the Island under any Circumstances longer than three Days for I can steadfastly believe before a Man could be starved so much as to eat Lizards he could not be able to catch them'.

As to ships or boats passing near enough to see any signal from the island, Lieutenant Salmond and the master of the *Frolic* reported that their parties saw none at all. Another officer saw two vessels pass, of which one might have seen a man waving; the others each saw three vessels, but thought none of them were near enough to see a man waving or signalling.

A modern [1978] description of Sombrero island shows that the observations of the naval search parties in June 1810 were accurate enough:[4] 'There is no beach, no tree, bush or shrub on the island, but the occasional stunted prickly pear can be seen, together with ground trailing plants that appear to thrive on sea spray. There are three species of lizard on the island, of which the most common is large and slate black in colour, running to 12 inches in length; and at least seven different species of sea birds which nest on the island in large numbers between May and July, their eggs providing the main source of food for the lizards...'

Of all the witnesses who had been discovered, or had come forward, George Hassell the Marblehead seaman was the first so far to say much that was positive and helpful about Robert Jeffery's whereabouts. The Admiralty sent a copy of his deposition to the Foreign Office, who referred it to the British Minister in Washington in the United States to make enquiries.[5]

The operation to find Jeffery had now become worldwide and the trail was rapidly growing warmer. Before any response came from America, and even before the Sombrero search got under way, news arrived from two widely separated places.

Much the more important came from Corunna, in Spain. At last Captain John Dennis of Marblehead, who had rescued Jeffery in his schooner *Adams*, had made himself known and made a brief sworn statement on May 19, 1810 before James Magniac, the British vice-consul there.[6] In it he put all the essential facts beyond doubt. He had seen from his vessel a man on Sombrero waving; he was brought on board the vessel so exhausted he could not speak, and when somewhat recovered gave his name as Robert Jeffery, a seaman of HMS *Recruit,* commanded by Captain Lake, and said he had been eight days on the island. Jeffery had recovered and went to Beverly, Massachusetts, where he lived and worked at his trade of blacksmith.

Immediately after Captain Dennis had made this statement, he happened to be standing alongside another American merchant captain at the landing place at Corunna, both waiting to return to their vessels at anchor offshore. Seeing a British naval captain stepping into his boat, the two Americans asked if he would take them as their ships were lying close to his own, HMS *Dryad*. The *Dryad*'s commander, Captain Galway, agreed, and on the way the conversation turned to the Sombrero case. To Galway's surprise, Dennis told them that he was the man who had rescued Jeffery and had sworn a statement before the consul.

Galway promptly reported this to his senior colleague, Captain Meads of *Arethusa*. The statement had been witnessed by other Royal Navy captains, but Meads was sceptical enough to summon them to his ship, together with John Dennis, whom he questioned in their presence. Then he sent for the deposition which had been left in charge of the master of a transport ship for transmission to the Admiralty, and compared it with the notes of Dennis's answers to his questions.

Meads duly informed his admiral, Lord Gambier, that what Dennis had said on the two occasions did in fact correspond.[7] Meads said he felt it necessary to report all the detail, 'the credibility of evidence generally so much depending on time, place and circumstances'. Cautiousness - or officiousness? It is hard to say; but Dennis must have been a patient man.

A few days later on the other side of the world, in Trinidad, another American witness appeared.[8] Early in June Admiral Cochrane in his flagship *Neptune* visited Trinidad which had been captured from the Spaniards only 13 years earlier, in 1797. An officer of Cochrane's squadron happened to meet Ambrose Martin, master of the Marblehead schooner *Polly*. Martin was brought before a member of the Council of the colony, John Nickell, who was also Alcalde (mayor or chief local officer) of part of the island.[9]

In his deposition, made on June 10, 1810, Ambrose Martin said that in May 1808 he had been in Marblehead when Captain Dennis's schooner *Adams* arrived from the West Indies and landed a man who said he was from the west of England, and had been put ashore on Sombrero from a King's brig. Although he had forgotten the names of the seaman and the naval captain, the details he did remember put it beyond doubt that Jeffery and Lake were those concerned. Jeffery had told him he had been on the island eight days, and had lived during that time on shellfish and eggs, and had drunk 'the Dew, Grass and the buds of Bushes'. He appeared in good health, and Martin had certainly not heard him say anything about eating his own flesh. He believed Jeffery was now living about 20 miles from Marblehead.

Captain Martin had sailed from Boston about February 28, 1810 and arrived at Trinidad about May 8. Alongside this statement in the deposition was placed a note 'This part must not be published as it will subject the Deponent to a severe Penalty if known at Boston that he had broken the Embargo'. Cochrane must have felt that this contribution would go some way to re-establishing his stock with the Admiralty, especially since the search of Sombrero had not yet begun. At length occurred the event everyone had been waiting for - the reported discovery of Robert Jeffery alive and well in America, and a statement in his own words.

This time it was the British Minister Plenipotentiary in Washington, Francis James Jackson, who took the initiative even before the Foreign Secretary, the Marquis Wellesley (eldest brother of the Duke of Wellington), had got round to sending him a copy of the statement made by George Hassell of Marblehead and asking him to make inquiries in America.[10]

Even then the authorities with one accord seem to have played down the Sombrero 'transaction' as they called it. In a curious process of delegation, Ambassador Jackson asked the pro-consul at Boston, W S Skinner, to 'obtain evidence of Jeffery's existence'.[11] Skinner in turn passed the job on to a Mr J. Ramsey, whom he described only as 'a Gentleman well known to me, & in whose examination the greatest Confidence may be placed'.

Ramsey followed the trail to Wenham in Essex County, Massachusetts, where he found a young man who was working there for Ziell Dodge, a blacksmith, and who readily answered to the name of Robert Jeffery.[12] On June 17, 1810 in answer to his questions the young man, who gave his age

114

as 21, made a statement describing in detail the Sombrero incident.[13] Invited to sign it, he did so with the cross used by those who were unable to write. Nevertheless Ramsey was satisfied that he had found the right man and took the declaration to the consul's office, where his own signature was authenticated by pro-consul Skinner. The document was forwarded to the British embassy in Washington.

The consul or his deputy, Skinner, summoned Jeffery to his office at Boston. There he arranged for the young man to acknowledge his declaration on oath before a local magistrate, William Stephenson, on July 14. The British Minister had already sent on the document to London. The news - but not apparently the text of the declaration - was published in the London newspapers on August 9. However the whole document was sent to Whitbread by the Admiralty.[14]

William Cobbett, the radical journalist, had attacked the Government about the Jeffery case since the court martial in February 1810. He reported at length in his *Political Register* the trial, the documents laid before the House of Commons and the debate. In his issue of August 18, following the Government's disclosure that Jeffery had been found and had sworn an affidavit, Cobbett wrote a scathing editorial, pointing out that it was Sir Francis Burdett whose motion had initiated the inquiries now being made. Had it not been for Burdett, he claimed, Jeffery's mother would probably never have heard of him again.

Cobbett announced that he would not be convinced of the truth of what was reported from America until he had seen the British Minister's report and examined it well. The best thing would be to bring Jeffery home to England. There could be only one objection, namely that Jeffery might be resolved never to risk being pressed again into the navy. 'Where he is now (in the State of Massachusetts it is said) he cannot be exposed to death for having taken a drink of spruce beer that did not belong exclusively to him. Where he is now, in short, if he has not both liberty and property, the fault is his, and not that of anybody else.'[15]

FAR in the western ocean
Sombrero rock does lie,
Where my hard-hearted captain,
Left me to pine and die.
Tho' sorrows are past describing,
Which on this place I felt,
And to relate my suff'rings,
The hardest heart would melt.

The rock was wild and barren,
No food I there could find,
And lest I should be starved,
With horror fill'd my mind.
I could not help despairing,
Nor safely could I sleep,
For fear of alligators,
Dread monsters of the deep.

For eight long days most wretched
An exile I remain'd,
Till by a friendly vessel,
I liberty regained.
'Twas Providence sustain'd me,
While on the rock I lay,
Or sure I must have perish'd,
Ere I could get away.

Now I am safe returned,
Unto my native shore.
To Heaven I'll be thankful,
And go to sea no more.
May God forgive the captain,
And cause him to relent,
And of this cruel action,
In sorrow to repent.

Verses printed in the *Account of the Sufferings of Jeffery the Seaman*, 1810.

Chapter 9

'HE WAS LOST AND IS FOUND'

In that summer of 1810 the artist Joseph Farington, RA, was on a sketching tour in Cornwall.[1] At Polperro he stayed on August 31 at the Ship Inn. Remembering that this was where the now famous Jeffery the Seaman came from, he asked about him. All he spoke to still believed that Jeffery was dead and that reports to the contrary were put out by friends of Captain Lake with a view to ending the public outcry.

Next day Jeffery's mother Mrs Coad called to see the artist. No doubt she hoped that some good might come of telling her story to any influential London gentleman who seemed interested. Farington found her 'a woman of respectable appearance', though unfortunately for us he was a landscape artist and not interested in sketching her portrait. After she had told her story, no doubt for the hundredth time, she went home to fetch the letter which Samuel Whitbread had written to her husband.

This was dated April 23, and probably by now a little dog-eared.[2] In it Whitbread had said he had passed to Sir Francis Burdett and the Admiralty the letter which Zephaniah Job had written. He added that Coad could not make any claim for compensation 'for loss of his son's services' unless it was certain that Robert had died; and even then Coad's personal situation might well be forgotten in the storm over Captain Lake's crime. At that stage the Coads seem to have been as interested in getting a cash benefit out of the situation as in young Robert's safety.

Mrs Coad said she and her husband now intended asking Whitbread's opinion of the reports alleging that Jeffery was still alive. Farington tried to comfort her by saying that in his view the newspaper reports alleging that the young man was well and settled in America seemed to be authentic. The main facts of the Sombrero incident, after all, had been confirmed now by many people. As late as June 20, when most of the activity was taking place across the Atlantic, a former shipmate of Jeffery's in the *Recruit*, an Irishman, had written to the Admiralty from Plymouth giving his own account of the landing whose outlines were now familiar[3]; but his letter was not made public.

From Honor Coad's point of view, two things made her sceptical of even the statement alleged to have been made by her son himself. First, there were the several conflicting stories put about in the past year, in more than one of which Robert was said to have died after appalling sufferings. Second, if he really had recovered and had been living all this time in America, why had he not written to her? Had she also known that the declaration made in America had been signed with an 'X' although Robert when he left school was perfectly able to read and write, she would have been even more disturbed. Lacking this knowledge, she still wondered whether the news from America was the cruel trick of an impostor, possibly even put up to it by Captain Lake's powerful family. And if the man found really were her son, was he coming (or being brought) home?

Mrs Coad wrote again to Samuel Whitbread who replied on September 9 to assure her that he, at least, had no doubt of her son's being alive, 'but it is extraordinary that he should not have written to you'.[4] Whitbread promised to press the Admiralty and was as good as his word, but between the slowness of communications and the authorities' lack of sensitivity there was little comfort to be gained from this quarter. Croker, the Secretary, wrote to Whitbread on September 11, saying in part, 'Jeffery's Mother ... seems to say that nothing but a Letter from him will satisfy her. I have no such letter to send you; and have only to assure you, that we have received official information of his having been living and well a few months ago, in America; and I have also some reason to expect that he will at no great distance of time, come to England.'[5]

Whitbread duly sent on to Mrs Coad this honest, but scarcely informative or helpful, letter. In fact, the British authorities, now convinced and relieved that Jeffery had been found were taking steps to repatriate him. In a letter to the Admiralty on July 14 enclosing a copy of Jeffery's statement, the pro-Consul at Boston had commented, 'I shall have great satisfaction in facilitating the return of Robert Jeffery to his Country and friends, of which he is very desirous. I am the more anxious to effect this, finding that he is living in this Country under the Patronage of those whose Politics and principles are inimical to Great Britain and I count the Honor of my Country engaged to accomplish it by the first favorable opportunity.'[6]

After several sessions at the Consulate, in the course of which Jeffery doubtless sought and was given assurance that he would be protected if he returned to England, it was arranged that he should be given a passage home in a warship. He was, after all, still technically a seaman in the Royal Navy.

First he was put on board a merchant ship lying in Boston harbour, bound for Halifax, Nova Scotia - British territory. When he arrived he reported to the secretary of the naval commander there, Admiral Sir Borlase Warren, and was given accommodation in the flagship, the 74-gun *Swiftsure*. Before long the schooner HMS *Thistle* was ordered to sail to England with dispatches, and Jeffery was put aboard her.[7] They made what was considered a quick passage, of 22 days, and arrived at Spithead on October 17, 1810.

During that passage, however, more well-meaning busybodies approached Mrs Coad who, with no letter or recent news of her son or indeed any firm statement that he was being sent home, became more and more agitated. The press relations of the British government were primitive and for some reason the text of Jeffery's declaration made in July had not been issued. The information that Jeffery had been discovered and had made a statement had been published in August 1810. Since then there had been no more news of him, and it was now mid- September. On the evening of September 11, the postman delivered to Mrs Coad's cottage a letter from a man named Noel Thomas Carrington, a former naval seaman turned schoolmaster and poet who a year earlier had opened a private academy at Plymouth Dock (now Devonport).[8] Carrington said he wrote at the request of 'several gentlemen of this town' to ask whether Mrs Coad had received any letter from Robert 'as it appears that he was a particularly dutiful and affectionate son, and one who let slip no opportunity of writing to you while on board the *Recruit*, it is probable that, if living, he has written to you; and this, of course, would place the fact of his existence beyond doubt.' This, incidentally, is the first we have heard of letters written by Jeffery from the *Recruit*; one would like to know what they revealed.

It is hard to believe that Mr. Carrington's concluding apologia, 'rest assured that nothing but a participation in that lively interest in the fate of your son, which pervades all parts of the British Empire could have induced me to have intruded on your time', was anything but hypocritical publicity-seeking. The letter can hardly have been better calculated to play on the poor woman's anxieties, for it reflected them completely.

She replied politely enough, perhaps helped by Mr Job, to say that she had heard nothing except what had appeared in the papers.[9] So long a time had elapsed since the published brief report based on the despatch from Washington that 'my doubts had overcome my hopes'. If Robert were alive, certainly he would have written to her; if he were really present when the alleged statement was made in America, 'they would have pressed him to write to me to convince me and the public of his existence'. She had asked to have a letter sent to him but had had no response. She enclosed the copy of the latest Admiralty letter which Whitbread had sent to her (and which Mr Barrow, the Secretary, had certainly not intended for publication).

It may be that once more the Jeffery case had been used as an

Opposition stalking-horse, and that Carrington and his friends had expected just such a reply, which they were waiting to send to a suitable newspaper. At any rate Carrington, signing himself A Constant Reader, sent the correspondence to *The Courier*, which published it in full on September 20.

Intended or not, at long last this stirred the Government into issuing to the press the text of Jeffery's declaration. *The Courier* printed it on September 27, *The Times* on the following day and Cobbett's fiercely radical *Political Register* on October 6. The document contained little which the public and Mrs Coad did not already know. What was now apparent, however, was that Jeffery had signed it with an 'X', which set the ball rolling once more in a way which might have been foreseen. Jeffery himself, of course, was en route for home although this was unknown to the British public or even to his family.

William Cobbett used the fresh topicality to the full, with an outburst in the *Register*,[10] 'every circumstance tends to heighten the horror which every good man will feel at this deed, committed, observe, not by one of the "rabble"; not by one of the "mob"; not by one of the "swinish multitude"; not by "a jacobin or a leveller"; but by "an Honourable Captain Warwick Lake"; by the son of a Lord, whose family have a large pension, paid by the people....'

The Government should show its disapprobation of the 'tyrannical act' and make all the amends it could. Let it be clearly understood, Cobbett emphasised yet again, that it was Sir Francis Burdett who had brought about the discovery of Jeffery, and the opportunity of doing him justice. Whitbread's part was blandly ignored.

The story now took another unexpected turn. When Mrs Coad saw the text as published, she might have been expected to show relief and compassion. Instead, having seen that the affidavit had been signed with a cross, she expressed complete disbelief that the declaration was made by her son at all. She sat down and with who knows who helping her composition and

121

penmanship wrote a long letter to Mr Carrington on October 4 which he made sure was published widely in the press on the 9th.[11] She wrote bitterly, 'Of course, you and the country will be now satisfied, that, from such information there can be no doubt of his existence. I have now no doubt myself but that some one has been examined, as therein stated; but I am persuaded that the Officers of our Government (who in this transaction appear to have done their duty) have been imposed on by that **** [the editor must here have deleted a libellous reference to Lake]. The story is plausible, and calculated to give weight to the testimony; for myself I believe it is collected from the evidence given on Lake's trial, and the subsequent examination of my boy's shipmates, &c.

'There is one thing that forcibly strikes me that it is a fabrication - that is, the signature to the Affidavit is a cross... My son could write not only his name, but a tolerable hand for a labouring youth, and understood the first rudiments of arithmetic, sufficient for his employment, and kept the daily journal of his work done in the shop. While there remains a doubt of his existence, why not have got a letter for me from him?

'Why not have pressed him so to do; or to let me hear some circumstance of his family or of his neighbours, something ever so trivial, not public? Or tell me how a letter might be conveyed to him, to convince me he really exists?'

Certainly the Government was lacking in human sensitivity or, if you will, a sense of public relations, in just the ways Mrs Coad suggested. Cobbett made the most of the opportunity in further vitriolic articles in his *Register*. Why had Jeffery, being safe in America, not sought justice against Lake from the British Government? Why had he come forward after all this time?

Cobbett extrapolated the situation,[12] 'if we suppose imposition in one case, we may in the other; if we suppose that a false Jeffery was brought forward by some unknown hand, it is very easy to conceive that John Dennis, Master [of the rescuing schooner *Adams*] might be prevailed upon to aid in the charitable deed'.

It must be shown that Dennis mentioned the matter when he landed Jeffery at Marblehead; could he have done so without the thing 'making a noise' throughout the whole of North America? Nobody had named the newspaper which was supposed to have reported the arrival. In short, nothing but the arrival of Jeffery in England and the affidavits of his relations and neighbours as to his identity would satisfy the public that he was alive and did not perish on Sombrero. Mrs Coad was 'in very penurious, and even distressed circumstances' and might possibly be prevailed upon to discontinue her complaints and to say that she had now heard from her son.[13]

That lady, poor though she may have been, had rather spoiled the impression of pure mother-love by a later paragraph in her letter perhaps written at her husband's instigation,[14] 'My present husband put my poor boy's life on the premises we now inhabit, purchased the ground, on which he built a dwelling-house and work shop, and holds his lease on the dropping of three lives - so that when the other two drop, it would be necessary to prove the existence of my son, or render the lease to the Lord of the Manor'.

A local farmer in Cornwall, perhaps John Richards of Port Looe who had previously been in touch with Whitbread, saw this letter and went to Polperro to see Mrs Coad and ask whether she were really the author of it.[15] No one was believing anyone else at this stage. She admitted it and showed Richards her growing collection of letters from MPs: one from Sir John Sinclair, 'a curious one', thought the farmer, two from Samuel Whitbread and one from John Curwen. He also called on Edward Rundle, the Polperro schoolmaster (later at Looe), who said he could swear to Jeffery's being able to write a good hand. The farmer then reported this in a letter to the *Morning Chronicle*. It was published in that newspaper in a slightly sub-edited form, a sentence in which the writer inveighed against the 'ruinous system' of the Government being removed, as was also the name of the arch-radical Cobbett.

The sensation was kept going to the last, and some of the participants - although well-meaning - were a little slow off the mark. At this stage some unnamed person remembered a letter he had received from Marblehead, written by a relative named Strawbridge as long ago as March 8, 1808, two and a half years before. Somewhat inaccurately, it described the rescue of Jeffery and his arrival in America. The anonymous recipient now showed the letter to a friend of his, the Rev John Evans of Islington, in north London, who promptly reported it, not to Mrs Coad, but to *The Times*. It appeared the day after Robert Jeffery's arrival in England.[16] Had the Admiralty thought fit to tell anyone they were bringing him home, or when he arrived, much of the furore would have been avoided.

Letter-writing about Jeffery had become a national pastime. The Islington parson, after receiving a visit from a naval officer who had come to England in the *Thistle*, wrote to a Sunday paper with a long quotation from the book of Job (not Mr Job of Polperro) and moral reflections about the providence of God from which officers should learn never to abuse their authority.[17]

Meanwhile in the late summer of 1810 Charles Morgan Thomas - never one to let well alone - made an even wilder accusation against Admiral Sir Alexander Cochrane, expressing his belief that the admiral was 'in the pay of the French government and a traitor to his country'.[18] This time, however, he made his charge in a letter to the Admiralty.

Thomas, though he may never have known it, now came within an ace of prosecution for criminal libel or an action for damages which would have completed his ruin. Cochrane's brother Basil took up the cudgels on the admiral's behalf. Attorney General Sir Vicary Gibbs was consulted, and in a short but interesting legal opinion came down in favour of a civil action.[19] The general idea was that any proceedings should enable Cochrane's character to be cleared publicly in court and as expeditiously as possible. Gibbs would have preferred a criminal information, to be laid by himself ex officio and leading to a trial in the King's Bench. This procedure could be used where senior officers of the Crown were libelled concerning their duty, and had the advantage of cutting out an initial hearing by a grand jury. However, to support such an information, said Gibbs, the admiral would have to provide an affidavit refuting the facts on which Thomas based his accusation. Without such an affidavit, Thomas could be tried only by way of indictment (that is a hearing by a grand jury followed by an ordinary criminal trial by a judge and petty jury). Truth is no defence to a charge of criminal libel, so that even if Thomas were tried on indictment he could not attempt to justify his accusations and so no evidence could be brought to refute them.

If instead the admiral brought a civil action for libel, Thomas could plead justification, and this, the Attorney General thought, would 'better answer the object of Sir Alexander Cochrane's friends'. That object, presumably, was to provide Thomas with enough rope to hang himself. In the event Sir Alexander did submit an affidavit, and the Admiralty went so far as to lend it to Basil, together with the original letter from Thomas.[20]

For whatever reason, no action, criminal or civil, seems to have been taken against him; nor do the letter and affidavit appear to have been returned. The Admiralty does not seem to have been tempted to give any credence to Thomas's accusations, and for the rest the Cochranes probably felt it was a case of least said, soonest mended. It was all very well for the Attorney General, but Sir Alexander must have regarded with apprehension the thought that Thomas might have a chance to vent his pent-up malice in any court. In the absence of the letter and the affidavit, little more can now be said.

Chapter 10

'TO GO WHERE HE PLEASES'

Samuel Whitbread hurried down to Portsmouth (taking the opportunity to visit some prison ships) and went on board the *Thistle* at the first opportunity. He wrote at once, on October 18, to Mrs. Coad to give her the first joyous news, and - as he hoped - to settle all doubts,[1] 'I have been on board... and have seen him in good health and spirits; he says he has almost forgotten how to write, that he sent a letter to you by a friend of his from America some months ago - that he got his master to write the letter - that he made the deposition which you have seen, and put his mark to it....From the description you gave me of your son, and the conversation I have had with him, there cannot be the smallest doubt of the identity of the man, and I congratulate you on his safe arrival in perfect health.

'He is under the care of the Admiralty, and will, no doubt, speedily visit you; but he will, probably, not remain long at this port, and expressed a wish that you should not be put to the trouble and expense of a journey to see him.

'I told him I would write to you today...'

The mystery of the 'X' signature was later explained a little further.[2] Jeffery, who, like the British authorities, cannot have foreseen the significance attached to the point, said reasonably that he had signed with a mark because it was the usual practice of seamen to do so, it being the least trouble. He had apparently written two letters home. Because of the American embargo on shipping, which everyone seems to have overlooked, the first one never arrived and the second was delivered to his mother the day after he came home.

Soon after Whitbread left, two other visitors arrived aboard HMS *Thistle*: Captain Lake's solicitor, a Mr Tatham, and his clerk named Davis. After spending some time with Lieutenant Peter Proctor, the schooner's commander, they had Jeffery called to the cabin. Tatham introduced himself and said he had brought Jeffery's discharge from the navy. The lawyers then took him ashore to Admiral Sir Roger Curtis, the Commander-in-Chief at Portsmouth, who signed the discharge dated October 21, 1810 [a Sunday]. It contained the significant phrase 'to go where he pleases'.[3]

An up-to-date description of the young man appended to the discharge certificate indicated that he had actually grown in height during his three years away, 'Robert Jeffery is five feet eight inches and a half high, is of a fair complexion, with light hair, and aged 22 years next Christmas; by trade a blacksmith; a mole on the left side of his navel, and one below it.'

Lieutenant Proctor had not spoken to Jeffery during the three-week passage, which despite the officer-lower-deck gulf seems both churlish and lacking in curiosity. However, it looks as if the navy at last had grasped that anything to do with this young man could still be a political hot potato. Jeffery afterwards said that on their arrival at Portsmouth the lieutenant asked him if he had spoken to him during the passage, 'his reasons for this I know not'.[4]

Next day, Monday, October 22, the lawyers took Robert Jeffery to London in a post-chaise, perhaps the first time he had ridden in one, to Mr Tatham's house near the Strand (probably a building where he had his office at Lincoln's Inn). There 'I was introduced to an old gentleman, who felt glad I was alive, and shook me by the hand. I understood he was a relation of Capt. Lake, and that he wished to give me something for my sufferings. A long paper was brought to me to sign, the subject of which was, that I would *not prosecute the Captain*: at last I consented to sign, after £600 was given me.

I was led to believe that, if I did not take that, I should get nothing. So I thought I was to make the best of it.

He added, 'I was promised, at the same time, that my mother should be made happy; and that whenever she wrote, she should be relieved; and, particularly, that a situation should be provided for MYSELF, to the amount of fifty or sixty pounds per annum!'[5]

After this adroit little exercise the solicitors and their clients no doubt felt happy that all had gone according to plan. To the Lakes, the money, a considerable sum, was well spent. The sooner Jeffery was out of town away from the reporters and politicians the better. It was also in the Lake family's interest as well as his own that he should arrive in Polperro with his fortune in compensation intact. So Jeffery was sent to Cornwall in the care of Davis, the solicitor's clerk.

No doubt again they travelled by post-chaise, the cost of which would in due course appear on the solicitor's bill. On the way Jeffery and his escort, probably of much the same age, got on well together. The clerk disclosed that his master, Mr Tatham, and his friends knew of Jeffery's arrival within 12 hours of his reaching Spithead and immediately set off to bring him to London. 'I therefore had no opportunity of landing out of his company', Jeffery explained afterwards, lest he be taken for a gullible bumpkin.[6]

In spite of the apparent generosity of the terms, it is significant that he was given no opportunity of receiving independent advice, something of which even Whitbread does not seem to have thought. Cobbett, as one would expect, pointed it out later on. He suggested that, because the lawyer was reported to have taken the view 'that one so inexperienced should not be trusted by himself with a large sum of money', a court of equity might overturn the compromise (on the ground of undue influence).[7] That might have been made a most interesting Chancery suit, but who would have guaranteed the costs? For Chancery delays were notorious and the outcome would have been uncertain.

Wigley's Rooms, Spring Gardens Passage, London
British Museum

Samuel Whitbread MP
National Portrait Gallery, London

Polperro, view from south (above)
and from the north (below) in 1810
engraved by W. Woolnoth after Joseph Farington

Polperro harbour with schooner visible beyond Peak Rock (above)
and (below) fishermen on the main pier passing the time of day.
Photographs by Lewis Harding c1870

A view of Sombrero today, showing the lighthouse
Vince Cate

The *Times* report (below) in May 1998 of plans to site
a rocket launching pad on Sombrero (see page 142)

Sombrero's remote location has made it an ideal home for rare nesting birds

Concern at plans for Caribbean rocket pad

BY NICK NUTTALL AND MICHAEL BROOKE

A ROCKET launching pad is being planned by the Government in the British territory of Anguilla to the outrage of conservationists.

The scheme, construction of which is expected to start early next year, is aimed at cashing in on the growing

concerned that this development will devastate what is one of the largest seabird colonies in the Caribbean."

Betty Anne Schreiber, a leading ornithologist at the Smithsonian Institution and president of Seabird Research in Alexandria, Vermont, said

of Dallas, Texas, which has pledged $250 million (£150 million) to build and launch commercial rockets from the island within the next two years. The company, owned by the American private bank owner and entrepreneur Andrew Beal, has hired a 50-

It was Thursday, October 25 when, somewhere along the road between Plymouth and Polperro, the two travellers met Jeffery's stepfather, Benjamin Coad, the blacksmith.[8] Word of their coming perhaps had preceded them or else it was a lucky chance and a surprise for both parties. Happily Coad recognised his stepson at once and rode on before them and down the hill into Polperro to forewarn Robert's mother.

Probably as he went he called out the news to the neighbours he met along the narrow Talland Street. It was six in the evening when Jeffery and his escort arrived to a tumultuous welcome. When the first excitement had begun to subside, people began to ask each other who was the young man with Jeffery. Word got round that the escort was a representative of the wicked Captain Lake, enough to rouse the Cornishmen to look on him with what *The Times* correspondent called 'apparent suspicion, and some degree of hostility'.

The clerk might well have found intimidating the murmuring of this hostile crowd whose reputation for violence as smugglers he must have known. However, he had made friends with Jeffery on the journey, and when Robert assured the neighbours that Davis was a friend and 'had taken the trouble of so long a journey for the purpose of protecting him' this was accepted, and the clerk was then 'received with respect and kindness'.

At last the party came face to face with Robert Jeffery's mother who had been so reluctant to believe that her son was really alive. Now, after only half an hour's notice that he was on his way, 'at first she gazed on him with a kind of bewildered anxiety, as if doubtful whether she could trust what she saw'. In a few moments she recovered herself, and they ran into each other's arms. 'Oh, my son' and 'Oh, my mother' interrupted by sobs on both sides, were all that they could utter for some time. At length the agitation of their feelings subsided 'and a scene of calm endearment ensued'. Mrs. Coad confided that when she first heard that her son had been left 'on a rock' she often prayed that God would allow his ghost to appear to her in dead of night so that she might know he was out of his misery.

Everyone in Polperro was caught up in the rejoicing, and crowds stayed up celebrating until late at night. Jeffery, now on top of the world, and his 'compensation' in hand, declared repeatedly that he entirely forgave Captain Lake and 'could take him by the hand with sincere goodwill if he were on the spot'. The clerk, Davis, stayed up with Jeffery until one in the morning, and after a few hours' sleep set off back to London next day.

Nowadays the media would not have been content even with so graphic account of the reunion. Cheque-book journalism would have secured Jeffery's story and his face would have become familiar to all through television. There were, however, two contemporary equivalents which *The Times* pointed out on the very day the young man arrived at Polperro,[9] 'Some of the industrious gentlemen who snatch at every opportunity of turning a penny, it seems, were extremely anxious to get possession of Jeffery, for the purpose of exhibiting him at a certain price of admission. The Admiralty, aware of the improper use that might be made of this poor fellow, gave him his discharge from the navy, on condition that he should immediately proceed to his mother in Cornwall. Had he remained in town, it is not improbable he might have been persuaded to appear at one of other of the twelvepenny debating shops. His sufferings would have furnished a copious theme for the vehement eloquence of the doctors of these schools.'

William Cobbett, despite his radical rhetoric, was realistic enough to accept that Jeffery's identity was now beyond doubt. From what had been published in most of the newspapers, 'it is not, I think, to be doubted, that this poor fellow is actually alive, and arrived in England.'[10] Writing from a cell in Newgate where he was serving a two-year sentence for criticising the flogging of mutineers, Cobbett could not resist sniping the Tory press,[11] 'Neither Nero nor Louis XIV was ever guilty of an act of cruelty surpassing that of the landing of Jeffery; and for this act it is, that the *Morning Post* is making an apology. (This was in reference to an obscure remark that 'it appears that the circumstances of this man's case have been greatly misrepresented'.) 'What has Buonaparte to do, in answer to all this print's charges of cruelty against him, but to remind it of its apology for Lake?'

In a period before illustrated newspapers, let alone television, the public were curious to see what the 'Governor of Sombrero' looked like. A crude and melodramatic portrait was hurriedly prepared showing a rather podgy Jeffery reclining on a low cliff waving his hand, apparently as night was falling or dawn breaking.[12] Copies were engraved and published in November, 1810 by 'C. Chrippes' of 16 Piazza, Covent Garden.

Jeffery soon found that, having signed the agreement not to sue for damages, the promises of continuing largesse from the Lake family were conveniently forgotten. 'Finding no farther notice was taken of my mother, or of me, some gentlemen of Polperro, wrote to the parties to know what more they meant to do - The Answer returned was, "IT DEPENDS UPON THEIR FUTURE CONDUCT". I then, of course, supposed that this was the manner after which they originally intended to fulfil the contract.'[13]

If Jeffery had harboured any doubts about making the most of his transitory fame this high-handed threat removed them. He went back to London and agreed, as perhaps the solicitors had anticipated, that a portrait of him should be featured at a London exhibition hall with personal appearances in addition. Ironically, the exhibition hall - Wigley's Rooms, a small-scale Olympia or Earl's Court - was in Spring Gardens, just across the Mall from the Admiralty. Their Lordships must have been distinctly annoyed.[14]

The Times, perhaps at the instigation of the exhibition promoters, had to retract their statement that it had been a condition of Jeffery's discharge that he should immediately leave London. They printed the text of the discharge certificate with its categorical statement 'to go where he pleases'.[15] As Cobbett remarked, the Lords of the Admiralty had no power, nor would they have attempted, to impose a condition.[16]

It had also been said that by the agreement he signed in exchange for the £600 he had bound himself 'not to exhibit his person'.[17] He denied later that he had signed any contract preventing him from exhibiting his picture and said the only paper he had signed was an agreement not to prosecute Lake. He took the opportunity to point out that from the time he landed he saw none whom he could consult except 'Captain Lake's friends'. If he had, he continued, he would have acted very differently for a British jury would have awarded him a much larger sum. 'Let the reader place himself in my situation, and say whether I am in *any wise* culpable in making the *present exhibition* of MY PICTURE? It is the only mode left me of supplying the deficiency.'

The Admiralty 'most honourably' paid Jeffery his back wages, but even a period of almost three years was not enough for more than a tiny amount to have accumulated, at £1. 16s 6d a month.[18]

A broadsheet account of the events to date was apparently compiled just after Jeffery's arrival in Polperro, which it dates as 'Monday last' (October 22, 1810). A single copy is known to exist, now in private custody. This may possibly be a reprint, or even a cutting, from a newspaper, but the writer - perhaps a journalist who 'covered' the event - claims that its account was confirmed by Jeffery himself. Much of the wording can be traced to the 'declaration' which he made in Amnerica, and had been published by Cobbett earlier in the month.

Booklets were produced to sell in conjunction with the exhibition. The first of these ran to 32 pages, and was 'printed for the author' and sold by Chrippes of Covent Garden who had been responsible for the crude engraving published in November. The booklet was entitled, 'Jeffery the Seaman, being a Narrative of his feelings and sufferings during his abode on the desolate Island of Sombrero, where he was left by the inhuman order of his Captain. Together with a Journal or Diary during the eight days he remained there. Interspersed with Strictures and comments on the conduct of Capt. Lake, well worthy of the attention of the British Legislature and the public in general. London, printed for the Author and sold by G. Chrippes (etc.)'.

The exhibition went on for at least six months. What seems to have been the next booklet produced was a quite short one, printed and sold by 'J Pitts', of 14 Great St Andrew Street, Seven Dials.[19] This was both maudlin and comic. Its title-page bore a crude woodcut of a man and a ship, and announced that the contents of the booklet were extracted from 'A JOURNAL OR DAIRY' of Jeffery's ordeal: probably one he had compiled for the purpose. The 'dairy' (correctly spelled in the text) was prefaced by a copy of his American affidavit which was followed by an account of the Polperro reunion plus two sets of verses of which McGonigall would have been proud (one is reproduced on page 116).

A fresh portrait, an excellent and perhaps flattering one, was painted by an artist named E M Jones, copies of which were later engraved by James Godby and published by the artist.[20] I have not succeeded in identifying Jones, but Godby was a prolific engraver who flourished about 1800-1820, then living in Norfolk Street, at the other end of the Strand from Spring Gardens. He published prints of works by Cipriani, Angelica Kauffmann, Sir Thomas Lawrence and even Raphael as well as many lesser painters.

The Jones portrait of Jeffery appears also to have been used as an illustration to a new booklet published in May 1811, printed by R. Edwards of Crane Court, Fleet Street and 'sold by Robert Jeffery, at his exhibition, Wigley's Rooms, Spring Gardens; B. Crosby, stationer, and by all the booksellers in the United Kingdom.'[21] The title-page bears the quotation: 'He was dead and is alive again. He was lost and is found' (Luke, xv, 20).

This was a much better production altogether. Its 32 pages contain a full version of the 'diary' of the eight-day ordeal on Sombrero, together with appendices giving a great deal of relevant documentation almost like a blue book. It states that 'the ...memoirs have been written under the immediate inspection of Robert Jeffery, and with no other than a few verbal alterations.' There is no reason to doubt this; the booklet was evidently produced with his co-operation and dedicated by him to Captain John Dennis of Marblehead, Sir Francis Burdett and Samuel Whitbread.

A handbill dated May 27, 1811 shows that the exhibition still continued, with admission price one shilling, and a picture still apparently being displayed by Jeffery in person.[22] This picture is fully described, and does not correspond with either of those mentioned above:

'A representation, large as life, of Jeffery landing on the island of Sombrero by order of Captain Lake. The *Recruit* brig, is at a distance; the small boat having put Jeffery on the rock, is returning, whilst the Victim, with fixed eyes and clasped hands, is seen in an agony of Distress!!!'

Its whereabouts, if it still exists, are unknown.

Chapter 11

EPILOGUE

When the exhibition eventually closed Robert Jeffery returned to Polperro. With the money he had made added to the sum he had received from the Lake family he is said to have bought a trading schooner, or at least a share in one. The venture apparently failed and he returned to his trade as a blacksmith.

Unlikely as it sounds, *The Times* reported on March 29, 1814 that Jeffery had turned up serving in the North Devon Militia, then stationed at Gosport, Hants. The war was not yet at an end and the militia were still recruiting. Sure enough, the muster rolls of the regiment show a Robert Jeffery having been recruited on March 19 (qualifying for £5 5s levy money) and serving as a private from the following day. He continues in the muster rolls until July 1814; Then there is then a gap in the surviving records; and when the series resumed in June 1815, the regiment being then at Plymouth, Jeffery's name no longer appears. (A Private John Jeffery was already in service when this Robert Jeffery was recruited, and was discharged on October 11, 1815.[1]) No other details are given; as *The Times* report of the enlistment was so nearly contemporaneous, it may well have been true; but equally some enterprising local may have jumped to conclusions because of a coincidence of name.

In 1818 he married a local girl named Elizabeth Scantlebury at Lansallos church.[2] His fame had lasted locally for a note was put in the marriage register, 'this is Robert Jeffery left on the Is. of Sombrero.' Two years later he died, of consumption according to Dr Thomas Quiller Couch. The fortunes of the other players in the drama were as varied as the people themselves.

Captain John Dennis Jr, of the Marblehead schooner *Adams* which rescued Jeffery, remained at sea. After the *Adams* he sailed in the brigantine *America* in 1815, and later as mate of another brigantine named the *Joseph*. He died in 1818, the subject of a romantic story told by a descendant.[3] Dennis had married in 1804 and he and his wife Deborah are said to have lived in a mansion near the shore with a turret into which Mrs Dennis would climb to watch through a telescope for the captain's return from sea.

One day as Deborah was ironing a shirt ready for her husband she left the room for some reason. On her return she saw on the ironing board her husband laid out in the shirt. She fainted, and her sister and mother came to her side. That night or the next day, Deborah again climbed to the turret to watch for her husband's ship. When it came in she saw the flag at half-mast. John Dennis had died of yellow fever at Martinique.

As for ex-Captain Lake, his friends in high places made sure that his disgrace did not last for ever, if only for the sake of his family. In 1815 he was given a commission as a lieutenant in the 7th Foot (the Royal Fusiliers) by the special instruction of HRH the Commander-in-Chief (the 'Grand Old' Duke of York).[4] The appointment of an unfortunate man named King was ordered 'not to take place' to make way for him. Perhaps this was done at the behest of the Prince Regent out of past friendship for Lake's father. The idea may have been to get him out of the country. If so it came to naught for he was soon transferred to the half-pay list.

In 1832 Lake was appointed Royal Agent for Van Diemen's Land (Tasmania), and he formally left the army. In 1836 he succeeded his brother as the third Viscount Lake, succeeding also to the £2,000 pension granted to their father for his distinguished services in India. Lake died in 1848, survived by a widow. There was no living male heir so the title became extinct.

Of the other officers serving in the *Recruit* on Sombrero day, December 13, 1807, Lieutenant Higgins, as we have seen, was drowned in August 1810 - apparently having made no statement other than those contained in his log, which survives, and his letters to his sister, which presumably do not. Lieutenant Mould, the second lieutenant, who was in charge of the boat which landed Jeffery, seems to have escaped all blame. After serving in the East Indies, he was based on Cadiz until November 1812, then after seven months was appointed to the *Clarence*, which served with the Channel Fleet and paid off in August 1814. His active service (still as a lieutenant) concluded with a four-month stint in HMS *Swiftsure*, also with the Channel Fleet, until she paid off on August 31, 1815 at the end of the war. He was still living in 1843 when he was made a commander on the retired list.[5]

Edward Spencer, the master of HMS *Recruit,* was also without a ship when the navy was reduced after the end of the war. He died in the summer of 1838.[6]

Towards the end of the Commons debate in April 1810, Whitbread had withdrawn his motion calling for an inquiry into the conduct of Admiral Sir Alexander Cochrane on an understanding that the Admiralty would call upon Cochrane for a further explanation. No such explanation appears to have been made public, nor apparently was Whitbread notified of one, as surely he would have been. It seems likely that the matter was conveniently shelved.

After the United States declared war on England in 1812 and invaded Canada, Cochrane was given the command of the North American station in 1814 and was active in directing the unsuccessful operations against Baltimore and New Orleans.[7] When peace came he was put on half-pay, but in 1821 was appointed commander-in-chief, Plymouth. He died unexpectedly in Paris on January 16, 1832 and was buried there in the Père Lachaise Cemetery.

Of the political personalities, two were to die tragically within a few years. Prime Minister Spencer Perceval was shot dead in the lobby of the House of Commons on May 11, 1812 by an insane man with a grievance. Samuel Whitbread died by his own hand, at his London house in Dover Street, on July 6, 1815.

The third politician closely connected with Jeffery's case, Sir Francis Burdett, lived to rejoice at the passing of the Reform Acts and remained a Member of Parliament until his death on January 23, 1844.

Charles Morgan Thomas, the eccentric purser through whom the story was revealed, went abroad and disappears from the scene. He is last heard of in November 1813 when he reclaimed his discharge papers from Whitbread 'as I am now about to leave the Country'.[8] The MP sent back the papers by return of post, and received a polite note of thanks.[9]

HMS *Recruit,* which had a short period of distinction under Napier, was sold in 1822. The buyer was recorded as R Forbes, but of the ultimate fate of the sloop there is no word.

Robert Jeffery's story and the events surrounding it were well publicised at the time, as we have seen. It continued and still continues to hold a fascination and from time to time has been written up afresh. Jonathan Couch included an account of it in his *History of Polperro*, edited by his son Thomas Quiller Couch and published in 1870. This in turn was a rich quarry for the author of a long article on Polperro in Charles Dickens' magazine *All the Year Round*.[10] In general the material was repeated without addition or detailed criticism.

Chambers' *Edinburgh Journal* draws attention to the more mysterious aspects of the story, 'in concluding this curious history, we wish we could authoritatively explain what may seem to require clearing up. We have heard that the tomahawk handle turned out to be part of a fisherman's hatchet; and it was surmised that the pair of trousers never belonged to Jeffery at all. Perhaps the signing of a mark was the effect of a memory caprice. Beyond this, after a diligent search, we are unable to discover any explanation of the circumstances which, for the time being, produced so much perplexity. If this were a fiction, it would have been easy to have invented a key to the letter: as it is, we leave it to our readers.'[11]

Those words were written a mere 40 years after the event. There is still less hope today of clearing up any mystery, if mystery remains. It would be a remarkable twist if the young man found in Massachusetts were an impostor, accepted thankfully as he was by the Government, by the Lake family and finally by Jeffery's own mother and step-father, each for their own ends. That such a deception could be maintained so widely and for so long seems most unlikely, but even if it had been the situation which gave rise to it was real enough, and the fate of young Jeffery could have been even more terrible.

So what good came of it all? It is tempting to reply 'not much', or at least much less than might be supposed. Yet who can tell? It must be remembered that punishments which now would be considered brutal were accepted as part of service life, and so continued long after Robert Jeffery's day. Theory of reform ran ahead of practice, and the number of old school conservative officers, and the lack of supervision made even agreed change difficult to enforce.

A new edition of the Admiralty regulations in 1806 instructed the captain,[12] 'not to suffer the inferior Officers and Men to be treated with cruelty or oppression by their superiors. He alone is to order punishment to be inflicted, which he is never to do without sufficient cause, nor ever with greater severity than the offence shall really deserve.' For all the good such well-intentioned but vague instructions did Jeffery, they might never have been written.

The practice of 'starting' was officially forbidden in 1809 but went on long afterwards. Flogging continued for another half-century. Cases of despotic and cruel captains were rare but they did not disappear overnight. At least they could no longer occur so easily without publicity or with impunity.

Robert Jeffery was an ordinary Cornish boy, not even a good seaman and his behaviour was far from perfect. Yet just because he was so ordinary a wartime 'Jack Tar' when the nation's dependence on its navy was obvious, consciences were perhaps stirred so that political reform came a little more quickly.

In 1811, when Jeffery was still exhibiting his picture in London, a British geologist visited Sombrero and found considerable deposits of phosphates. They lay undeveloped, however, for another half century, during which time the sea-birds and lizards had Sombrero to themselves.

With the increase in number and size of merchant ships using the Anegada Passage the need for a light on Sombrero became urgent.[13] This was reported to the Admiralty in 1848 but nothing was done. Eleven years later a Royal Mail steamer, the *Paramatta*, was wrecked there with considerable loss of life.

The United States claimed possession of the island, one result of which was a new American survey of the island in 1859, afterwards used by the British Admiralty as the basis for its chart published in 1868. It must have been at this period that names were given, probably by the American surveyors, to the main coastal features of the island. The origins of these names are probably already forgotten, and only one brings to mind the ordeal of Robert Jeffery: 'Spencer Point', on the south-western side of the island. The master of HMS *Recruit* who wanted the boy put off the ship was, of course, Edward Spencer. The choice must be a coincidence; it would be ironic if that man's name had been perpetuated while the landing of Jeffery at a spot not far to the north remains uncommemorated.

After eight years' disputation the American claim was amicably settled and the British Treasury sanctioned the erection of a lighthouse. A metal girder lighthouse was built and came into operation on New Year's Day, 1868. By that time desolate little Sombrero was humming with an different sort of activity which made the light even more essential.

After the American civil war ended in 1865 large areas of the United States had been were being opened up for agriculture and there was heavy demand for fertiliser. Americans came to Sombrero and for about 20 years from 1860 they exploited the phosphate deposits, paying an annual rent of £1,000 to the British Crown Agents for the Colonies, subsequently reduced to £500 on appeal to the House of Lords. The barren rock was equipped with a light railway, a steam rock crusher and accommodation for the workers, with loading points set up on the shoreline. By 1870 some 3,000 tons were being shipped each year.

The phosphate was found in pockets in the rock which could be worked only by blasting. When surface reserves had been exploited the Americans turned to the sea. Now divers had to drill holes underwater and insert blasting charges. After the explosion, loosened portions of rock were hoisted to the surface, an enormously expensive operation that could not be carried on indefinitely. By 1890 production had fallen greatly so the workings were abandoned. The graves of seven workers who died there can be seen today.[14]

Sombrero is now administered from Anguilla, which broke from St Kitts in 1967 and is now a self-governing dependency of the United Kingdom. The lighthouse, which had been run by the American phosphate company, was taken over by the British Board of Trade in 1893. It had a staff of four keepers and a cook who spent six weeks at a time on the island, latterly in touch with civilisation by radio and relieved from Anguilla by helicopter. Even so, their life in a hurricane area is described as 'arduous and lonely', with spray blowing as high as the light tower. The 1960 hurricane 'added to the already barren appearance of the island by scattering the many rock dumps of the old phosphate workings, by damaging many of the old workers' buildings, and by creating a scene of utter desolation which is the impression gained by the visitor who visits

Sombrero today'. Considerable further damage was done in January 1977 when exceptional swells caused waves to break over the rock cliff to the north-west, demolishing a row of buildings once used to accommodate the phosphate workers, scattering the debris and wrecking the landing crane.

A new lighthouse again constructed of metal girders came into operation in 1962. Its beam was an important navigational mark for international shipping, including supertankers passing from the Atlantic to the Caribbean through the Anegada Passage. The light station was transferred in 1983 to Trinity House, which commissioned and presented to Anguilla in 2001 a new, automated replacement, with a 60-foot high fibre-glass tower. The Government of Anguilla issued a commemorative set of postage stamps, showing all three lighthouses, in 2002.

The wildlife of this tiny island is important because of the endemic black lizard and the bird population. A survey in 1998 found hundreds of brown boobies, brown noddy terns, bridled terns and sooty terns nesting there, together with about 50 pairs of masked boobies, scarce in this region. Frigate birds roost on the island, but apparently do not nest there.

Sombrero is no longer unspoiled although just as lonely and barren as when Robert Jeffery was marooned there. It says much for the survival of natural species that the birds and lizards, which had the 95-acre island to themselves until man came to exploit it in the last century, are still numerous. In 1997 an American company, Beal Aerospace, signed a 98-year agreement to use Sombrero as a site to launch commercial space satellites. Conservationists in the United States, Britain and Anguilla expressed concern. In the event the company did not proceed, and in October 2000 ceased business for other reasons.

NOTES AND REFERENCES

[Unless otherwise stated, numerical references refer to documents in the National Archives]

Chapter 1 THE ISLAND OF DOOM

1 Robert Jeffery was baptised at Fowey on January 22, 1790. The baptismal entry in the parish register is reproduced as an appendix in *A Narrative of the Life, Sufferings and Deliverance, of Robert Jeffery, 1811*, 'sold by Robert Jeffery ... and B. Crosby, Stationer' (hereinafter *Crosby Narrative*), p 21. On p 5 he mistakenly gives 22 January as his date of *birth*; it is more likely that a letter from Zephaniah Job dated April 21, 1811, among the papers copied in ADM 1/5402, is correct in giving December 11, 1789. In his own sworn statement made in June 1810, Robert said he had been born in Polperro: *Political Register* October 6, 1810, col. 561. The muster books of HMS *Recruit* give his age at entry into that ship as 18; in fact he was only 17.

2 *Crosby Narrative*, p 5; Job to Whitbread, April 15, 1810: court martial papers, ADM 1/5402; *The Farington Diary*, ed James Grieg, 1922- 28, vol 6, p 115. I have not discovered which of the Polperro public-houses was kept by Jeffery; when his wife re-married in 1801 she was described as 'of Talland' - in other words, the east side of the village. The little river Pol bisects Polperro, separating the parish of Talland from the parish of Lansallos.

3 Thomas Bond, *Topographical &c Sketches of...East and West Looe*, 1823, p 25.

4 *Crosby Narrative*, p 5. Jeffery, in *Crosby Narrative*, p 5, is again slightly mistaken on dates. He says his father died in 1802, but the date of his mother's re-marriage puts the death of her first husband prior to June 21, 1801.

5 Coad to Whitbread, April 17, 1810: Beds Record Office, Whitbread Papers, 5240. A rental of the manor of Rafiel (mostly on the Lansallos side) in 1806 shows a tenement let to Ben Coad, at 4s rent and 2s heriot, on the lives of himself, aged 44, his wife Honor, also 44, and Robert, aged 17: Frank H Perrycoste, *Gleanings from the Records of Zephaniah Job*, reprinted from the *Cornish Times* 1929, ca 1930, p 66; Perrycoste says he was unable to identify the house in question.

6 The *Lord Nelson* was owned in Plymouth, the principals being John Teed and Charles Martin. Her commander was Francis May; neither he nor the officers appear to have been Polperro men. Declaration for letter of marque, July 14, 1807: HCA 26/92.

7 James Greig (ed), *The Farington Diary*, 1922-28, vol 6, p 115. The rating of 'armourer' in the RN existed only in ships of 6th rate upwards.

8 Zephaniah Job to Samuel Whitbread, April 21, 1810: court martial papers, ADM 1/5402; Beds RO, Whitbread Papers, no 5243.

9 Log of the master of HMS *Recruit*, Edward Spencer: ADM 52/3856.

10 Graham Haslam, in *The Duchy of Cornwall*, ed Crispin Gill, 1986, p 42.

11 The facts of this incident as given by Jeffery in the *Crosby Narrative* and by the master, Edward Spencer (at the eventual court martial) substantially agree. Jeffery said he 'took up' a bottle of rum, while Spencer stated that he 'took out' a bottle with some rum in it. He was evidently seen with the bottle in his hands, and it would seem likely that he intended to replace it after his drink, rather than taking it out of the cabin. Jeffery incorrectly placed the incident before the ship reached Madeira, some weeks earlier than it actually occurred.

12 The punishments are recorded in the master's log, and likewise in the log of the first lieutenant: ADM 52/3856; and ADM/L/R/72 (National Maritime Museum), but not in that of the Captain. Curiously the logs make no reference to Jeffery being accused of theft, always a serious offence at sea.

13 As a result of subsequent events, the circumstances were recounted many times and minutely examined. Different versions agree in outline, if sometimes conflicting in detail. Jeffery's own first account is in his affidavit of June 27, 1810, printed in the *Political Register*, October 6, 1810, cols 561-562 and elsewhere; his later version is in the *Crosby Narrative*. Spruce beer, incidentally, was what the name implies: a drink made from fermented spruce or pine cones.

14 Bowen to Admiralty, June 20, 1810: ADM 1/4381, no 478.

15 ADM 52/3856.

16 Dudley Pope, *Life in Nelson's Navy*, edn 1987, p 171.

17 Job to Whitbread, April 15, 1810, court martial papers: ADM 1/5402; Beds RO, Whitbread papers, 5238.

18 For a description of Sombrero island, and its subsequent history mentioned later in this book, I have drawn upon a typescript information leaflet prepared by the Department of Trade in 1978, at a time when the Department was administering the Sombrero light as part of the Imperial Lighthouse Service.

19 ADM 52/3586.

20 My account of Jeffery's landing is based principally on the *Crosby Narrative* together with evidence at the court martial ADM 1/5402 (and published in the *Political Register*, March 17, 1810) except for details of which the source is identified as a seaman - these are from the letter by Peter Bowen to the Admiralty, June 20, 1810 (after the court martial): ADM 1/4381, no 478; or as otherwise indicated.

21 Lt William Millett of HMS *Aboukir,* to his brother, Thomas Millett jun, a surgeon, April 28, 1810: Beds RO, Whitbread papers, 5261.

22 Evidence of Edward Spencer, court martial minutes: ADM 1/5402 (and published in the *Political Register*, March 17, 1810.

23 Bowen to Admiralty, June 20, 1810: ADM 1/4381, no 478.

24 Evidence of Francisco Valla, court martial minutes: ADM 1/5402 (and published in the *Political Register*, March 17, 1810.

25 Long afterwards, when memories had begun to fade but interest in Jeffery's fate was at its height, other details of the scene were produced. One is contained in a letter from an un-named 'very respectable friend at Fowey' reprinted from a Truro paper by *The Times*, May 1, 1810, p 3, recounting details said to have been given to Jeffery's aunt, Mrs Anne Line, by Libby and Johns soon after their return to Polperro. It is poignant and graphic, but contradicted or unconfirmed by all other sources, including Jeffery's own account and the court martial evidence, which I have preferred. For what it is worth, it includes the following passage: '...Jeffery, when in the boat rowing on shore, desired them to drown him but they could not but must obey the Captains order. When the boat was on shore he clung to the boat. At last, a man forced him on the barren rock. They gave him the biscuits and beef. Lieutenant Mould would have given him money, but he replied it was of no use to him. He then gave him the boat hook and staff, three handkerchiefs, to hoist as signals: and after that they left him.' Another witness, John Marley, said that the quartermaster gave Jeffery a half-dollar: ADM 1/5402.

26 Job to Whitbread, April 15, 1810, court martial papers: ADM 1/5402; Beds RO, Whitbread papers, 5238; Lt William Millett in his letter to his brother, April 28, 1810: Beds RO, Whitbread papers, 5261, says that Libby, as a member of the crew of the captain's gig, was actually one of those who rowed Jeffery ashore. I have preferred Job's version; Millett did not know Jeffery [even being uncertain about his Christian name], but while staying at Lansallos, near Polperro, happened to hear Libby's story.

27 Lt William Millett to his brother, April 28, 1810: Beds RO, Whitbread papers, 5261.

Chapter 2 THE ADMIRAL'S BLIND EYE

1 Evidence of Sjt Thomas Jenkins, court martial minutes: ADM 1/5402; Cobbett's *Political Register* March 17, 1810, col 411.

2 Evidence of Edward Spencer, court martial minutes: ADM 1/5402; Cobbett's *Political Register*, March 17, 1810, col 410.

3 Nearly half a century earlier Sombrero was included in Andrew Brice's *The Grand Gazetteer*, Exeter and London, 1759, at p 1205 'Sombrero, a desert Caribbee Island, 30m NW of Anguilla. 80 NW of St Christopher, W lon 63 lat 18.30. 'Tis round, and had Name by the Spanish from a round Hill in the Middle, which gives it the Form of a Hat. It has the same Humming-birds &c. as Anegada.' Desert it was known to be; the existence of humming-birds at any period must surely be illusory.

4 Lt Millett to his brother [quoting Libby], April 28, 1810: Beds RO, Whitbread papers, 5261.

5 ADM 52/3836.

6 ADM 51/1805 [May 8, 1807-June 14, 1808].

7 ADM 52/3836.

8 Ibid.

9 Bowen to Admiralty, June 20, 1810: ADM 1/4381, no 478.

10 National Maritime Museum, ADM/M/R/72.

11 ADM 37/1716.

12 Court martial minutes: ADM 1/5402; Cobbett's *Political Register*, March 17, 1810, col 407; Navy Board to Admiralty, April 12, 1810: ADM 106/2250.

13 Navy Board to Admiralty, April 12, 1810: ADM 106/2250. Correct procedure for cancelling an 'R' was to add a note to that effect citing the order concerned.

14 Dundonald, Earl, *Autobiography of a Seaman*, 1860-1, p 28, quoted in Michael Lewis, *A Social History of the Navy 1793-1815*, 1960, p 167. These are the facts as stated by Cochrane, but Dr NAM Rodger, the naval historian, considers that at best they are only half true.

15 Cochrane to WW Pole, November 1, 1809: *Political Register*, March 24, 1810, col 463.

16 Evidence of Edward Spencer, court martial minutes: ADM 1/5402; *Political Register* March 17, 1810, cols 401-402.

17 Cochrane to Pole, November 1, 1809; *Political Register*, March 17, 1810, cols 463-4.

18 Court martial minutes: ADM 1/5402; *Political Register*, March 17, 1810, col 408.

19 Lake to Admiralty, August 17, 1808, enclosing survey report: ADM 1/2077, no 10.

20 Ibid, muster book of HMS *Camilla*: ADM 37/886.

21 Lake to Admiralty, September 19, 1808: ADM 1/2077, no 11.

22 *Parliamentary Debates*, April 3, 1810, vol 16, cols 448-9.

23 *Navy List*.

24 ADM 9/8, no 2823.

25 Muster book of HMS *Recruit* ADM 37/1719.

26 Ibid.

27 Ibid.

28 Muster book of HMS *Camilla*: ADM 37/886; muster book of HMS *Princess of Orange*: ADM 37/667.

Chapter 3 'THE GOVERNOR OF SOMBRERO'

1 *Crosby Narrative* on which the story of Jeffery's ordeal and subsequent movements in this chapter is based. At the end of the first- person narrative [dated May 12, 1811] is on p 18 the note: 'The preceding memoirs have been written under the immediate inspection of Robert Jeffery, and with no other than a few verbal alterations. Thomas Brand. Hackney-road, April 28, 1811'.

2 B Lindsey, *Marblehead Sea Captains and the Ships in which they Sailed*, 1915, reprinted by the Marblehead Historical Society in 1981, gives a little information on John Dennis and the *Adams*.

3 P S Lord and V C Gamage, *Marblehead*, Radnor, Pa, 1972 (updated), p 16.

4 Massachusetts volume, *American Guide* series, 1937, p 27.

5 Brief descriptions of places outside Marblehead in which Jeffery worked are based on those in the massive *History of Essex County*, Boston, Massachusetts 1878.

Chapter 4 A PECULIAR PURSER

1 Cochrane to Admiralty, August 4, 1809, enclosing extracts from Thomas's letters, ADM 1/330, no 20, copy enclosed (together with copy of Thomas to Pole, September 7, 1809) with Barrow to Whitbread, 27 April, 1810: Beds RO, Whitbread papers, 5251; Admiralty to Samuel Whitbread, MP, 27 April, 1810, 'A Statement of what is known in this office of the case of Charles Morgan Thomas...': Beds RO, Whitbread papers, no 5250.

2 Ibid. Thomas himself said he 'applied to' the flagship captain, not to Cochrane's secretary; even if this be accepted, the point would still remain valid: Bristol *Mirror* May 5, 1810, p 1, cols. 1 and 2.

3 Thomas to Whitbread, May 8, 1810: Beds RO, Whitbread Papers, 5263.

4 Ibid. Thomas says he was 'some time a prisoner' on board the *Dart* and *Port d'Espagne* before joining the *Pelorus*.

5 Thomas to Bathurst, March 24, 1810: Cobbett's *Political Register*, 17 March, 1810, cols 398-9. Copies of this and other documents were also printed by order of the House of Commons, in HC Accts & Papers 1810, (208), XIV, 149. For the *Star*, see ADM 1/5405, court martial of Concanen.

6 RTB Fulford *Samuel Whitbread 1764-1815*, 1967, p viii; Thomas to Whitbread, May 11, 1809 and June 8, 1809: Beds RO, Whitbread Papers, 5137 and 5137.

7 Lake to Pole, July 3, 1810: Cobbett's *Political Register*, March 24, 1810.

8 Daly v Rolles, cited in the *Narrative*, pp 26 and 27; a lengthy report can be found in the Courier of 21 April, 1810, p 2, cols 3 and 4, where it is given [evidently in the context of the Jeffery incident] without date, as if it were current news. The captain, John Rolles, far from being dismissed the service, eventually became Rear-Admiral of the Red.

9 Admiralty to Whitbread, 27 April, 1810: Beds RO, Whitbread papers, 5250; Thomas to Admiralty, September 7, 1809, Ibid, 5251.

10 Cochrane to Admiralty, August 4, 1809: ADM 1/330, no 20; copy enclosed with Barrow to Whitbread, 27 April, 1810, Beds RO, Whitbread Papers, 5251.

11 Thomas to Admiralty, September 7, 1809: Beds RO, Whitbread Papers, 5251.

12 Thomas to Admiralty, September 27, 1809: ADM 1/5054.

13 ADM 1/5399.

14 Ibid.

15 ADM 1/5402.

16 Admiralty to Whitbread, 27 April, 1810, Beds RO, Whitbread Papers, 5250.

17 Thomas to Admiralty, 10 November, 1809: ADM 1/5054, no 87.

18 Cobbett's *Political Register*, March 24, 1810, cols 463-4.

19 Ibid, cols 461-2.

20 Ibid, cols 462-3.

21 Admiralty to Whitbread, 27 April, 1810, Beds RO, Whitbread Papers, 5250.

22 Moses Greetham was Deputy Judge Advocate of the Fleet from November 6, 1804 until his death on July 23, 1831: ADM 6/29 fo 2, and naval salary and pension books (at Ministry of Defence naval history library), vol XIV fo 15, both cited by JC Sainty, *Office-holders in Modern Britain IV, Admiralty Officials 1660-1870*, 1975. Curiously, Sainty gives no holder of the superior office of Judge Advocate of the Fleet between 1768 (Jackson) and 1824 (Twiss), but Nathaniel Bond is so styled in the *Law List* for 1810. A Moses Greetham, son of Moses, was admitted to Gray's Inn in 1781, but the *Law List* for 1810 gives no counsel of this name; presumably he changed to the other branch of the profession and is the Moses Greetham listed as notary and attorney at Portsmouth in the latter year. On Greetham's death in 1831 the office of Deputy was abolished.

23 Greetham to Croker, January 15, 1810: ADM 1/4633, no 32.

24 Curtis to Admiralty, January 20, 1810, enclosing one from Lake to Greetham of the same date: ADM 1/1148, no 147a.

Chapter 5   DISMISSED THE SERVICE

1 The court comprised, in addition to the President, Captain W Bedford, Captains Charles D Pater, John E Douglass, John Barrett, Sir A C Dickson, Bt,

Richard H Pearson, Richard Ragget, Robert Plampin, Thomas Rogers, John Irwin, Hon Charles Paget, William Cumberland, and Robert Hall. Court martial minutes, ADM 1/5402 printed by order of the House of Commons as HC Accounts and Papers 1810 (72), XIV, 129; also reprinted in Cobbett's *Political Register*, March 17, 1810. The account of the court martial in this chapter is based on these minutes.

2 ADM 1/5402, ADM 12/27d.

Chapter 6 POLITICIANS' FIELD-DAY

1 *The Times* February 7, 1810, p 3.

2 *The Times* February 13, 1810, p 3.

3 *Hansard, Parliamentary Debates* vol XV, cols 424-6.

4 *Commons Journal* vol LXV p 100.

5 *Commons Journal* vol LXV p 122. The minutes were printed as HC Accts & Papers, 1810 (72), XIV, p 149.

6 *Political Register* March 17, 1810, col 397 [Thomas to Bragge-Bathurst]; and March 24, 1810, cols 460-4 [remaining papers].

7 *Hansard, Parliamentary Debates* vol XVI, cols 426-49.

8 Before a person could be tried for a serious crime, it was necessary to have a preliminary hearing by a grand jury (as is still the practice in America). If the grand jury were satisfied that there was a prima facie case against the accused, they would find a true bill; if not, be would be discharged. Grand juries were abolished in England for most purposes in 1933, and completely in 1948.

9 *Crosby Narrative* pp 23-4.

10 William Cobbett (an opponent), in *History of the Regency and Reign of George IV*, 1830 p 77.

11 The classic case of a conviction for murder without a body is Rex v Perry in 1660. John Perry, of Chipping Campden, Glos, confessed that he, his mother and his brother had committed a murder and hidden or destroyed the body. On the basis of this confession al three were convicted and hanged. Two years later the 'victim' returned with a story that he had been kidnapped and sold to Turkish pirates: J Gordon Stanier in *Law Times* 25 Feb, 1955; 14 State Trials p 1312.

12 Coad to Whitbread, April 17, 1810: Beds RO, Whitbread Papers, 5240.

Chapter 7 WITNESSES GALORE

1 Burdett to Whitbread, April 23 and 29, 1810: Beds RO, Whitbread Papers, 5244 and 5241.

2 [Dr] Oke Millett jun to Whitbread, April 9, 1810: Beds RO, Whitbread Papers, 5237, and copied in ADM 1/5402.

3 Frank H Perrycoste, *Gleanings from the Records of Zephaniah Job of Polperro* (reprinted from the *Cornish Times*), c 1929, p 86 and *Some Records of Talland Parish*, (reprinted from the *Cornish Times*) c 1930, pp 52-3. Apparently at Lansallos the Rev Mr Millett succeeded in 1804 a man named Lake - but this at least must be a coincidence.

4 Post Office RO, Freeling letter-books, vol 23, pp 478-9.

5 Job to Whitbread, April 15, 1810: Beds RO, Whitbread Papers, 5238; copy in court martial papers, ADM 1/5402.

6 *The Times*, April 19, 1810, p 3.

7 Barrow to Admiral Young, 20 April, 1810: ADM 1/5402.

8 ADM 12/141; ADM 1/5402 John Richards, a local farmer probably at Port Looe and perhaps something of a busybody, wrote to Whitbread on 28 April telling him of Sir John Sinclair's letter to Coad and also describing the summoning of Libby and Johns; Richards had apparently enlisted Whitbread's help in connection with certain Cornish rotten boroughs including Looe and Saltash, both controlled by the Buller family: Beds RO, Whitbread Papers, 5255.

9 Coad to Whitbread, April 17, 1810: Beds RO, Whitbread Papers, 5240.

10 Sinclair to Whitbread, April 26, 1810: Beds RO, Whitbread Papers, 5249.

11 Coad was referring to the fact that his cottage and workshop were held on a 'lease for lives', that is for a term (usually 99 years) or until the death of the last of three named people, whichever was the sooner. When any of the nominated people died a new 'life' could usually be substituted, but for this the landlord would charge a fine or lump sum.

12 Ryder to Admiralty, April 10, 1810: ADM 1/4213.

13 Job to Whitbread, April 21, 1810: Beds RO, Whitbread Papers, 5243; ADM 1/5402.

14 ADM 1/5402, Spencer to Croker, May 21, 1810 .

15 ADM 1/5402.

16 FO 5/73, fo 106-; copies also in ADM 1/5402 and in the Whitbread Papers [Beds RO], 5252-4 (with covering letters). Hassell said he had a wife and child at Marblehead. He had left that place on March 15, 1809 for Boston, where he shipped in the *Pocohontas*, Captain Zachary Hatwell, for Savannah and Liverpool. He arrived at Liverpool in July 1809, and after some time in Liverpool Infirmary he had joined the *Fame* belonging to Nielson and Heathcote, Liverpool merchants, in September on a round trip to Demerara, from which he had arrived back on 4 April. The boy whom he mentioned as having deserted from the *Recruit* was called 'Rapley or something like it': 'his Aunt keeps a Public House in Liverpool next door to the London Inn, in Redress Street'. I have been unable to identify the boy in question.

17 The 61-ton Marblehead schooner *Betsy*, Captain Christopher Francis, is recorded for 1809; in 1806 the same captain had a schooner named the Joseph: B J Lindsey, *Old Marblehead Sea Captains and the Schooners they Sailed in*, Marblehead Historical Society, 1915, rep 1981, p 53. [The same work gives 1810 for Captain Dennis's *Adams*, with a different vessel recorded for Dennis in 1807; so on dates the book cannot be accepted uncritically.]

18 Lt William Millett to Whitbread, April 28, 1810: Beds RO, Whitbread Papers, 5261.

19 According to the muster book John Marley, 145 Co, Chatham headquarters, joined the *Recruit* as corporal on May 24, 1807, was reduced to private on September 15, 1807, and promoted to corporal again on May 10, 1808; discharged to Antigua Hospital, August 15, 1808: ADM 37/1719.

20 Lt Manley to Admiralty, August 15, 1810: ADM 1/2163.

21 *The Times*, May 1, 1810, p 3.

22 ADM 9/8, no 2823.

23 Libby to Admiralty May 2, 1810: ADM 1/4833, no 167 .

24 Admiralty to Whitbread, April 27, 1810: Beds RO, Whitbread Papers, 5250 .

25 Ibid.

26 Thomas to Whitbread, April 24, 1810: Beds RO, Whitbread Papers, 5245.

27 Barrow to Whitbread, April 27, 1810: Beds RO, Whitbread Papers, 5251.

28 Eg in the *Bristol Mirror* April 28,1810, p 4, cols 1 and 2.

29 Thomas to Whitbread, April 29, 1810: Beds RO, Whitbread Papers, 5258.

30 *Bristol Mirror* May 5, 1810, p 1, cols 1 and 2.

31 Thomas to Whitbread, May 8, 1810: Beds RO, Whitbread Papers, 5263.

32 Thomas to Whitbread, 28 May, 1810: Beds RO, Whitbread Papers, 5265. Thomas had written to Whitbread on April 29 and again on 8 and 10 May, 1810: Beds RO, Whitbread Papers, 5263 and 5265, accusing Cochrane of various malpractices.

33 Thomas to Whitbread, June 8, 1810: Beds RO, Whitbread Papers, 5137.

Chapter 8 SOMBRERO RE-VISITED

1 Minute, dated April 11, on Ryder to Admiralty, April 10, 1810: ADM 1/4213. The formal answer of the King to the Addresses from the House of Commons was not delivered until June 7: CJ, LXV, p 468.

2 Cochrane to Hayes, May 31, 1810; ADM 1/331.

3 ADM 1/331, which includes Hayes' chart of the island with a sketch of the island's appearance - because of the supposed resemblance to houses - copied from one by Captain Hodge of the Surinam and individual reports of the officers in charge of search parties.

4 Typescript information leaflet prepared by Department of Trade in 1978.

5 Barrow to Hamilton, May 10, 1810: FO5/73, fo 104.

6 Published in *The Times,* June 13, 1810, p 3.

7 Meads to Gambier, May 28, 1810: ADM 1/143, no 225

8 Cochrane to Barrow, June 16, 1810: ADM 1/331. The letter was received on July 28 - a remarkably speedy passage.

9 ADM 1/331.

10 FO 5/69, p 7.

11 FO 5/69, p 369.

12 Ibid.

13 *Political Register* October 6, 1810, cols 561-2.

14 Croker to Whitbread, August 8, 1810: Beds RO, Whitbread Papers, 5268

15 *Political Register*, August 18, 1810, col 196

Chapter 9 'HE WAS LOST AND IS FOUND'

1 James Greig (ed), *The Farington Diary*, 1922-3, vol VI pp 115-6.

2 *Crosby Narrative* pp 26-7.

3 Bowen to Admiralty, June 20, 1810: ADM 1/4381 no.478.

4 *Crosby Narrative* p 27.

5 *Courier* September 20, 1810, p 2.

6 Skinner to Admiralty, July 14, 1810: ADM 1/3845.

7 *Crosby Narrative* p 14.

8 *Courier* September 20, 1810, p 2; DNB, sub nom.

9 *Courier* September 20, 1810, p 2.

10 *Political Register* October 6, 1810, cols 623-4.

11 Eg *Morning Chronicle* October 9, 1810, p 3.

12 *Political Register*, October 13, 1810 cols 623-4.

13 Ibid, col 624.

14 Ibid, col 619.

15 *Morning Chronicle* October 20, 1810, p 2; 'a reputable Farmer in the County of Cornwall' is the only indication of his identity given; but see Chapter 7, note 8. Rundle was the master of Speccott's School at Looe from 1811: HC 1837-38, xxv pt 1, p 513; perhaps he was previously assistant to Parnell who taught Jeffery or possibly he was teaching at the Polperro charity school and was a neighbour of the Jeffery family.

16 *The Times* October 19, 1810, p 3.

17 *The Examiner* letter dated October 25, 1810; *Crosby Narrative* pp 30-1.

18 Thomas to Admiralty, August 28, 1810 and September 7, 1810: entered in the Digest, ADM 12/145, but the originals are not to be found in the appropriate box, ADM 1/5054.

19 Opinion of the Attorney General, Sir Vicary Gibbs, dated September 5, 1810, enclosed with letter from Basil Cochrane to Croker, January 8, 1811: ADM 1/4428.

20 Minute on the letter of Basil Cochrane to Croker, January 8, 1811: ADM 1/4428, and enclosed receipt signed by Cochrane promising to return the letter and affidavit, or an attested copy should they be lodged in a court of law.

Chapter 10   'TO GO WHERE HE PLEASES'

1 *Crosby Narrative* pp 27-8 .

2 Ibid, p 19.

3 *Crosby Narrative* pp 15 and 21-2.

4 Ibid, p 15.

5 Ibid, p 16.

6 Ibid, p 14n.

7 *The Times* October 31, 1810, p 3; *Political Register* November 7, 1810, col 850.

8 *The Times* October 31, 1810, p 3.

9 *The Times* October 25, 1810, p 2.

10 Political Register October 31, 1810, col 769.

11 Ibid, October 31, 1810, col 777.

12 An example of the engraving is in the archive of the National Portrait Gallery, London.

13 *Crosby Narrative* p 17.

14 A brief description of Wigley's Rooms, and exhibitions held there, can be found in Walter Thornbury and Edward Walford, *Old and New London 1873-78*, vol IV, pp 82-3. The history of the Rooms is covered in the London County Council *Survey of London*, vol XX, 1940, pp 67-8. See also Richard D Altick *The Shows of London* Harvard UP, 1978, passim; Jeffery's exhibition seems to have eluded all writers on the subject, however. Houses were later erected on the site of Wigley's Rooms by Decimus Burton; these became the offices of the Metropolitan Board of Works and afterwards of its successor, the London County Council.

15 *The Times* November 6, 1810, p 3; the text of the discharge certificate is also printed in *Crosby Narrative* pp 21-2.

16 *Political Register* October 31, 1810, col 771.

17 *Crosby Narrative* p 16.

18 Ibid, p 25n.

19 A copy of this booklet is in the library of the Essex Institute, Salem, Massachusetts. Bibliographical details of this and the other booklets are given in G C Boase and W P Courtney, *Biblioteca Cornubiensis*, 1882, vol 1, pp 272-3, vol 3, p 1246.

20 Raymond Lister *Prints and Printmaking* 1984, p 204. Examples of the engraving are held by the National Portrait Gallery and National Maritime Museum, London.

21 A copy of this booklet is in the British Library, pressmark 1203.d.8/2; a photocopy is held by the Marblehead Historical Society, Marblehead, Massachusetts.

22 A copy of this handbill is in the Essex Institute library, Salem, Massachusetts.

Chapter 11   EPILOGUE

1 *The Times* March 29, 1814, p 3, quoted in John D Byrn, Jr, *Crime and Punishment in the Royal Navy* (*a study of discipline on the Leeward Islands Station, 1784-1812*), Gower Press 1989;   muster rolls of the North Devon Militia: WO 13/523.

2 Transcript of Lansallos marriage register, typescript, Robert Jago, 1981.

3 Information from a fourth-great grandchild of John Dennis Jr, kindly communicated by the Marblehead Historical Society, to whom I am also indebted for the information that the death at Martinique of John Dennis, 'mate of the brig Joseph, John Johnson Master' was recorded at Marblehead on October 11, 1818.

4 Commander-in-Chief's Memoranda, July 27, 1815: WO 31/424.

5 ADM 9/8, no 2823; Navy List.

6 His death was reported in the third quarter of 1838: Navy List.

7 The admiral's nephew Thomas, whom he had appointed flag-captain, became implicated in a Stock Exchange swindle. Although almost certainly innocent he was convicted and imprisoned. Disgraced in England, he

showed himself a great naval commander in the service of the liberation governments of Chile, Brazil and Greece. He was later pardoned, restored to his rank in the Royal Navy and in 1831 succeeded his father as Earl of Dundonald.

8 Thomas to Whitbread, November 16, 1813: Beds RO, Whitbread Papers, 5271.

9 Thomas to Whitbread, November 19, 1813: Beds RO, Whitbread Papers, 5272.

10 Typescript information leaflet prepared by the Department of Trade, 1978, when it administered the Sombrero light as part of the Imperial Lighthouse Service; Cdr R Langton-Jones, RN, *Silent Sentinels* 1944, pp 195-200.

11 One grave, with a stone deeply incised, presents a mystery. The young man buried there has not been traced in the records at St Kitts or neighbouring islands. The inscription reads:

In Memory of
SILVANUS WILLIAMS
Nephew of the late Dr. Benjamin Davis of
Regent Park College, London.
One of the Company of Revisors of the
Bible and Brother-in-law of
Mr Sutton, Swansea
Born 1st January, 1846.
Died 2nd January, 1876.

Regent's Park College, a Baptist institution, is now in Oxford. It looks as if Silvanus may have been a Baptist missionary in the West Indies, but how he met his death is not yet known.

12 *All the Year Round* September 13, 1873, pp 487-91.

13 Chambers' *Edinburgh Journal* vol 9, 1848, pp 150-1.

14 Quoted in Christopher Lloyd *The British Seaman* 1968; paperback 1970, p.218; upon which I have drawn for general information in this section of the chapter.

INDEX

THE AUTHOR

James Parkyns Derriman retired after a career in journalism and public relations to devote time to historical research and writing, specialising in legal and maritime history. For two decades he undertook part-time research work at The National Archives and elsewhere, for lawyers, academics and authors. His personal interest is in the history of the Looe and Polperro area of Cornwall, renowned for its smuggling and privateering exploits.

Marooned was his first full-length work in this field. Mr Derriman's forebears include RN officers from Napoleonic times onwards, one an admiral. He himself served in the wartime Merchant Navy which he entered as a deck boy after beginning his career as a cub reporter in London and Winchester, Hants. After the war he qualified as a barrister, then resumed his journalistic career in Fleet Street. In 1955 he moved into public relations with the J Walter Thompson Co and later joined the former Charles Barker Group to form a PR consultancy, of which he became joint vice-chairman, and then Company Secretary of this large British communications group.

In 1973-4 James Derriman was President of the professional body now the Chartered Institute of Public Relations, and he is an honorary vice-president of the European Confederation of Public Relations. He is a Freeman of the City of London.

His publications include:
Pageantry of the law (1955)
Discovering the law (1962)
Public relations in business management (1964)
Company-investor relations (1969)
The bridge-builders, joint editor (1980)
Marooned (1991)
Killigarth: three centuries of a Cornish manor (1994)
Chancel Repair Liability - how to research it (2005)

Reviews of *Marooned*

"A fascinating book which, like a few novels, is difficult to put down when you have started reading it... thoroughly recommended"
Journal of the Cornwall Association of Local Historians

"Well researched... and tells an interesting tale."
Mariner's Mirror

"A curious tale, well told by an ex-journalist and specialist in maritime history."
Cornish Guardian

"A 'horror story' and a true one."
The Naval Review

"Once started, the book is difficult to put down... in truth, stranger than fiction."
Cornwall Family History Society Journal

"Reveals far more of English society and its navy of Napoleonic times than a simple case of cruelty at sea... Recommended for those anxious to see more of the sailor's past world than seamanship, gunnery or the minutiae of shipboard life."
The Northern Mariner